M. G. Parameswaran, or Ambi as h
Strategist and Founder of brand-building.com, a brand advisory.
A large part of Ambi's illustrious forty-year career was spent in
advertising, first at Rediffusion and then a twenty-five year stint at
FCB Ulka. He has worked on iconic brands and companies such as
Tata, Wipro, Zee, TCS, Thermax, Indica, GSK, Tropicana, Abbott,
ITC etc.

Ambi now reads, writes, teaches and coaches leaders across
multiple domains. He is a guest faculty at IIM, Calcutta and IIM,
Ahmedabad and an Adjunct Professor of Marketing at SPJIMR.
His columns appear regularly in the *Business Standard* and the
Mint, in addition to other business magazines and dailies. He is a
distinguished alumnus awardee of IIT Madras, an alumnus of IIM
Calcutta (who served for ten years on its Board of Governors),
an AMP graduate from Harvard Business School and a PhD in
management from Mumbai University.

Ambi can be reached at ambimgp@brand-building.com; he is
active on LinkedIn and Facebook as Ambi Parameswaran and on
Twitter as @ambimgp.

ALSO BY AMBI PARAMESWARAN

FCB Ulka Brand Building Advertising: Concepts & Cases

Understanding Consumers: Building Powerful Brands Using Consumer Research

Building Brand Value: Five Steps to Building Powerful Brands

Ride The Change: A Perspective on the Changing Indian Consumer, Market & Marketing

DraftFCB Ulka Brand Building Advertising - Case Book II
(with Kinjal Medh)

Strategic Brand Management
(with Kevin Lane Keller and Isaac Jacob)

For God's Sake: An Adman on the Business of Religion

Nawabs Nudes Noodles: India Through 50 Years of Advertising

Sponge reads like a collection of short stories, masterfully crafted over a long and rich canvas of time — and distilled with key insights. Ambi has shared examples from a wide cross-section of products & services, presenting anecdotes and glimpses that keep the reader engaged and alert. A wonderful and easy read!

Vinita Bali, Former Managing Director,
Britannia Industries Ltd.

Sponge is a delightful book, because it narrates powerful human stories of leadership in such an endearing manner. Reading this book is like a nice lilting waltz through some of the most compelling lessons of management, all set to beautiful music in Ambi's inimitable style. If you are thirsting for new knowledge, sponge off this book shamelessly. It is such a compelling read.

Harish Bhat, author of *The Curious Marketer* and *Tata Log,* Brand Custodian, Tata Sons

There's so much you can learn by keeping your ears and mind open. Ambi Parameswaran's collection of client stories is rich and varied and his S.P.O.N.G.E. learning framework is something worth soaking in.

Anita & Harsha Bhogle, authors of *The Winning Way: Learnings From Sport for Managers*

Ambi has built this book around the concept of a sponge; one who absorbs good ideas and knowledge from others. That is a good way to live. For everyone you meet has something to teach you. And it is in your selfish interest to be humble, listen, and learn from every interaction. I assure you that reading Ambi's book will be a good use of your time, for you too can sponge some knowledge off one of the finest marketing thinkers that India has produced.

Amish, best-selling author

Ambi's latest book *Sponge* presents an interesting concept of how we can all become better leaders if only we listen to and learn from our clients and customers. Based on actual incidents and exchanges, the book is an easy read, and packed with some powerful lessons. Pick up a copy and get ready to soak in the lessons.

Sanjeev Bikhchandani, Founder and Executive Vice Chairman, Info Edge Ltd. (naukri.com)

SPONGE
Leadership Lessons I Learnt From My Clients

AMBI PARAMESWARAN

First published by Westland Publications Private Limited in 2018

61, 2nd Floor, Silverline Building, Alapakkam Main Road,
Maduravoyal, Chennai 600095

Westland and the Westland logo are the trademarks of Westland
Publications Private Limited, or its affiliates.

Copyright © M G Parameswaran, 2018

ISBN: 9789387894006

10 9 8 7 6 5 4 3 2 1

Typeset by Jojy Philip, New Delhi 110 015
Printed at Thomson Press (India) Ltd

*This book is dedicated to all those
wonderful clients from whom I 'Sponged'
so many valuable lessons.*

Contents

Introduction

'Uncle, Vikesh is a sponge,' said my nephew. And that term stuck like an earworm. A meme, as Richard Dawkins may call it.

The organism we call a 'sponge' (members of phylum Porifera) is indeed interesting to study and learn from. It does not have a nervous, digestive or circulatory system. Instead, it relies on maintaining a constant flow of water through its body to obtain food and oxygen, and also, to remove waste.

What an interesting organism! It just lets in water with all its nutrients, absorbs these nutrients to stay alive and uses the water to remove impurities from its body.

In contrast, the dictionary defines a 'sponge' as a 'person who takes advantage of the generosity of others, who absorbs, soaks up money or efforts of others'. Given this definition, we often refer to people who borrow with alacrity as 'sponges'. For a minute if we dismiss the negative associations that seem to go with the word sponge and look at the positives, is there something we can learn from the way a sponge behaves? Could we perhaps see the sponge as a person or a thing that absorbs good things freely? To make our work life better. To become better leaders. Better human beings.

The core idea of this book is based on something that I have attempted to practice all my life—the tenet that we could become better by listening, learning and adapting ideas, thoughts and actions from the wise people we meet in the course of our working life.

When you start your career in your early or mid-twenties, you perhaps wonder whom you could adopt as a role model. Who is that you can emulate and learn from?

You may or may not be able to find a mentor or a coach. You, and this is becoming increasingly true, may work under a series of superiors, most of whom are only keen on furthering their own career objectives. And bonus payouts!

Where then, do you turn for advice, counsel and feedback?

I discovered, early in my career that some extremely valuable lessons could be learnt if I just listened to and learnt from my customer interactions. Like it was for me, some of the most engaging conversations you might ever have in your life are likely to be with your most challenging customers. You can either dismiss them as a bad dream or you can use them as a springboard to improve yourself.

A quick tour through my career may help set the context. Having been brought up in a conservative Tam-Brahm family, I was given no option but to study engineering. Fortunately, I managed to do well in the Joint Entrance Exam (JEE) and joined Indian Institute of Technology (IIT), Madras. Soon I discovered, not too surprisingly, I was not going to make a good engineer. The way out was to do an MBA which I did at the Indian Institute of Management, Calcutta. During my summer internship I became acquainted with advertising and so I joined advertising in the year 1979, probably among the first of the IIT-IIM brigade to venture into that creative field. After three years at Rediffusion Advertising, I moved to marketing, first a six-year stint at Boots Company (handling brands like Brufen, Coldarin, Strepsils, Burnol) and then at UDI Yellow Pages as General Manager – Sales.

The itch to get back to advertising was too strong and I joined Ulka Advertising in 1989 and spent the next twenty-five plus years there, helping in the transformation of a struggling agency into one of India's best.

Through my first innings in advertising and my long second innings, I ensured that I was in touch with my clients on a 24/7 basis. The country changed dramatically from 1979 to 2016 and some of the stories here are from the early era (cigarette advertising was perfectly kosher then) and many are from the post-liberalisation era. Over this long innings in advertising, working with clients across India, I got to handle a wide range of products and services. Many brands I had the good fortune to work on went on to do very well in the market and some continue to do so. But more importantly, I got to interact with some really smart clients, who taught me a lot. Or should I say, I soaked up a lot from them like a 'sponge'.

When I did my Executive Coaching certification programme at the Coaching Foundation of India, I discovered that in coaching parlance, this is called 'Active Listening'. It is the kind of listening when all your senses are engaged in the process of listening. And if you approach each client conversation as an exercise in active listening and learning, you will come out a winner.

In whichever industry you may be working in—banking, media, IT services, real estate, durables—you will end up meeting customers every day. And each engagement with a customer can teach you something new.

I was fortunate to work with and engage with some highly respected names in the Indian corporate world. I learnt a lot from all those powerful conversations that I was privileged to have with such people. This book is an attempt to present those conversations in context. It is my interpretation and presentation of what I think I learnt from those conversations. I must have had more than a few thousand such powerful conversations in the course of my career. Many of those conversations have stayed with me and some are as fresh as if they happened yesterday.

What did all these conversations teach me? They taught me lessons on how to address a problem. How to get involved with the task at hand. How to motivate a team.

Many things came to light in the course of these conversations. The CEO of the biggest corporate group in the country was so passionate about the exact colour of the vehicle to be displayed at the car launch, to the extent that he researched the way that colour was to be used, and was willing to drop everything to check out the car, four hours before the launch.

The person running a large engineering company was interested in writing the body copy of a campaign, simply because he believed his inputs would be of value to the company, though it was definitely not his job.

The CEO of a large company was humble enough to travel halfway across the city, to meet a lowly executive to tell him that he, the CEO had been wrong and the executive correct in his evaluation of the trade situation.

And there are many stories like the ones above. All of them demonstrate things that a young executive or manager can learn from a seasoned business leader.

Through the various stories in the book I try and show how one can learn important managerial lessons and human development skills by both listening to the words of customers, and also 'listening' to what is left unsaid.

Some stories demonstrate the power of humility. Then, there are stories about how passion and attention to detail is a great strength found in leaders. Loyalty to one's business partners is yet another great virtue found in leaders, again something that is worth emulating.

Similarly, many more such virtues will be recounted through real-life anecdotes. Each chapter will end with some reference to work done in this area by management and behavioural science experts. For the enthusiastic reader, adequate reference is provided with each story.

The book through its many anecdotes will attempt to make some important points on how you can improve yourself, if you listen and learn through customer engagements.

You don't need a specialist 'Executive Coach' to help you improve your managerial and leadership skills. If you listen and learn, you can get 'coached' by your own clients. For free.

But to do that, your frame of reference has to change. You have to approach each client customer engagement not from the point of view of selling or a quick win, but from the point of view of what you could learn through the process of selling. You may actually end up selling a lot more as well. Also, chances are you will also emerge as a better leader, a better manager and a better person, in the bargain.

Becoming a sponge while interacting with a wise customer is something that can transform your life. Absorb the words of wisdom. Learn from their behaviour. Look beyond what is obvious. And like the colourful sponge inhabiting the ocean floors, you too will rid yourself of impurities and get enough nutrients for you to develop into a better leader.

I benefitted by becoming a SPONGE. You could, too.

The SPONGE
Learning Framework

As you get ready to read the twenty-five plus chapters of the book, I thought it would be a good idea to present a framework for learning. No prizes for guessing what this framework is called.

The SPONGE learning framework will help you deconstruct the stories and also evolve your own model of how you will learn from the hundreds of client and customer interactions you will possibly have every year.

S – **Super Active Listening.** By this I mean that not only should you listen to the words being said, but also the tone and manner.

P – **Probe and Question.** As you listen to the words, seek to probe and question why the person is saying what he or she is saying. Is there something that you are missing out, something that you did not understand?

O – **Observe and Note.** Don't just listen to the words. But try and figure out if there is something else in their behaviour that you ought to note. A CEO putting his arm around the shoulder of an engineer, for instance. What does that say or mean?

N – **New Behaviour to Emulate.** What is the new behaviour you have seen that you think is worth emulating in your own work or personal life? Is it the way a situation was handled? Is it the humility shown in an adverse situation?

G – **Getting to a Goal.** How will this new behavior help you achieve your life goal? How will it make you a better manager and a better leader?

E – **Expand, Enlarge, Share.** By sharing your learning from the various incidents you learn from, you end up remembering them for life. And hopefully you will help a colleague or a family member improve too.

So there you have it – S.P.O.N.G.E.

Get ready to SPONGE from my stories in the chapters to follow. You can read them in any order. But remember how the SPONGE Framework helped me decode behaviour and learn from it. You too can be a SPONGE in no time.

Happy SPONGEing!

A Shiny New Car

My secretary peeped in, interrupting me in a meeting. 'Mr Krishnan is on the line. He says it is urgent.' I dropped what I was doing and picked up the phone. 'Yes, Mr Krishnan, any problem?'

'Ambi, where are you?' Mr Krishnan asked, coming to the point right away. I replied that I was in my office at Nariman Point.

'Can you quickly go across to the Homi Bhabha Theatre at NCPA (National Centre for the Performing Arts)? I just got a call from the Group Chairman's office. He is leaving for the NCPA in five minutes. Unfortunately, I am at Andheri, doing a dealer visit and I can't get there in time.'

When I questioned Mr Krishnan about the reason for Mr Ratan Tata's visit to the NCPA, he replied that he wasn't sure. He did mention that Mr Tata wanted to check out the new car and so probably wished to go over the evening's launch programme as well.

I quickly put on my favourite blue jacket (something that I always kept in my office for such emergency meetings with heads of companies), and got to the NCPA in less than two minutes. In the short drive, I ensured that the Event Manager, Michael Menezes was also alerted about the visit of the Group Chairman.

Tata Motors was our agency's biggest and most prestigious account (clients are called 'accounts' in advertising agencies). We had launched the Indica and later relaunched it as the Indica V2 to much success. This was followed by the Tata Indigo, which went on to become the top-selling sedan. We were now getting ready to launch the Indigo Marina that evening. Thanks to some really smart engineering, the Tata Motors engineers had managed to create three different products on the same platform, well before the rest of the Indian auto industry managed to figure out the production and branding advantages such a strategy offered.

Indigo Marina was going to be the latest offering, a station wagon that offered a lot of storage space, while providing fantastic seating space and comfort. Riding on the success of Tata Indigo, it was felt that this car would be able to find ready acceptance and offer a choice to the value-conscious Indian car buyer, who was upgrading to a sedan.

The campaign was based on the consumer insight, 'More space gives you the freedom to do more with your car' and the tag line 'Carry your world with you', had been researched and found to resonate very well with potential car buyers. Dog lovers especially loved the idea that the dog could stay in the boot, but could be an active participant in the ride (by sitting in the back of the car, the dog could look into the rear seat).

When I reached the NCPA, the new Indigo Marina was parked outside Bhabha Theatre. Three engineers from the Tata Motors Pune plant were giving the car a last minute clean up. I alerted them about Mr Tata's visit and asked them why they thought he was keen on visiting the NCPA just then. In all our previous launches, Mr Tata had arrived only a few minutes before the start of the event and had never checked the venue or the car, ten hours before the launch.

Soon, I discovered the reason for his eagerness to visit the NCPA. And it had nothing to do with the NCPA and all to do with the car.

The engineers explained that at an international auto show, Mr Tata had seen a car that looked as if it had been 'electroplated'. He wanted his engineers to find out how it was done. Obviously, one cannot electroplate a whole car. So clearly, there was a different technology involved. The engineers did their research, but were pleasantly surprised that even Mr Tata had done his research and presented them with a way in which it could be done. Apparently, the electroplated look was obtained by using a particular type of material that then had to be polished and cleaned many times to get the shine.

The engineers were told that for the launch of Indigo Marina, the shiny electroplated car would be displayed. They too enthusiastically rose to the challenge, having never done anything like this in the past. Unfortunately, their experiments did not yield great results. In the weeks leading to the launch of the car they had failed several times. When Mr Tata had visited the Pune plant the previous month he had categorically rejected the car they had prepared, pointing out to the many yellowish patches on the car.

The engineers in Pune however, were a tenacious bunch. They did not want to give up. So the previous week they had managed to improve the methodologies and managed to get a car that looked splendidly electroplated. The marketing team loved the car and green-lighted it for the launch. But when Mr Tata heard that his electroplated car was ready for launch, he wanted to make sure it met his quality standards.

The team from Pune were worried that Mr Tata was coming to do a spot check of the car. They were reasonably sure that the new car would pass his test, but you can never be sure about what he will notice, they told me.

As we were going around the car, we noticed a Tata Safari driving in and Mr Tata got out of the car as soon as it stopped. The engineers from Pune knew him and more importantly, he knew them by their name.

They took him to the car and in what seemed to me like an hour, Mr Tata went around the car many times. He knelt down to inspect the lower parts of the car. And just as the engineers suspected, he did notice a small yellowish patch.

I was summoned and Mr Tata asked me how the car looked. I replied that the car looked splendid and a shiny electroplated looking car was indeed unique. He then asked me to go around the car to spot any blemish. I could not. At this stage, he pointed out the small patch he had noticed and asked if that would be noticeable by the audience. I replied in the negative.

Then he wanted to know about the launch event. I explained that it would be like a Broadway musical that would culminate in the grand unveiling of the car. Mr Tata wanted to know where the car would be parked on stage, whether it would be too far from the audience, whether its shiny exterior would be appreciated in all the light and smoke. The questions were only a few, but each of them was very incisive.

Luckily, my answers seemed to satisfy Mr Tata. He then proceeded to speak with the engineers from Pune. I could see their broad smiles as he complimented them for their work.

As Mr Tata left in his Tata Safari, I got the engineers to tell me the whole story and that was when I figured out why he had decided to drop everything he was doing to spend an hour inspecting the car, in the heat, outside the NCPA.

What did I learn from this episode? Why did Mr Tata make the trip to the NCPA?

Yes, Tata Motors and its passenger vehicles occupied a special place in his heart. But still, why, I wondered.

In his book *Fifth Discipline*, Peter Senge of MIT postulates five principles towards building learning organisations. The first principle is 'Personal Mastery'—the need for a leader to be the master of what he wants to perform.

The second principle is the need to have adaptable 'Mental Modes'—the ability to change and become more amenable to suggestions.

The third principle is having a 'Shared Vision' with the team since a leader does not achieve anything without the help of the team.

The fourth principle is the key principle of 'Team Learning'—how a leader has to ensure that this takes place regularly.

And finally, the last principle was how it was also important to see the 'organisation as a whole'.

The book continues to be a much-quoted book on organisational transformation and learning. And as we progress towards managing a floating population of millennial workers, managers would be well-advised to build a 'learning organisation'.

In the story of the shiny car, I discovered how Mr Tata was passionate about the business of cars—he was constantly learning new things about the business, he was ready to sit with his engineers to address a new problem, he was keen to follow through, not just make grand statements and he was ready to push the team and get pushed in the bargain.

In its essence, this story is all about the passion of the leader to visualise and execute a plan.

The story of the shiny car could also be seen as a metaphor for the larger problems business leaders have to handle every day. Clearly, what emerges is that it is not just enough to make statements, the important thing is whether you have it in your arsenal to carry it through and what you are willing to do to ensure that it happens.

Can you think of your own 'Shiny New Car' story, something that you too visualised and were keen to make happen? How far did you go to ensure that it happened?

The next time, you have a similar idea, what will you do to make it happen?

(*Postscript:* A story popped out of the *Economic Times* on 12 February 2017, more than ten years after the launch of the 'shiny new car'. The paper reported that Mr Ratan Tata had cancelled a visit to the UK due to the loss of his two German shepherds, Tango and Tito, who passed away in quick succession. The paper went on to say how Mr Tata accompanied his pets on their last journey in his Tata Indigo Marina, which had been customised to ferry his pets.)

Sages and Books

Sterling Resorts pioneered the concept of 'Time Share Holidays' in India. After a bit of a struggle, the founder R. Subramanian discovered in J. R. K. Rao a marketing strategist who could visualise how the concept could be sold to a very sceptical customer. During his tenure as the Head of Marketing at Sterling Resorts, JRK (as we called him) roped me in to help him create a parallel revenue stream for the company.

For the uninitiated, time share holidays are sold to customers as a lifetime of free holidays (one week per annum) for an upfront lumpsum payment. The important thing is that resorts are built by collecting money from customers. Hence, it is essential to have new customers sign on to ensure resorts continue to be built in newer locations, expanding the company's offerings and thereby, making the company an attractive choice for holiday-seekers. Sterling figured out early on that unless they gave the visiting families a great time, they would have poor word-of-mouth. And poor word-of-mouth would stop new enrollments. So JRK's remit was not just marketing but also customer experience. As he planned out the strategy he figured out that there would be empty slots in any resort's booking calendar.

In the hotel, hospitality and tourism industry, a bed not slept in, a seat not occupied, is a lost opportunity ('put bums in restaurant seats and bodies in hotel beds' is the mantra for better revenue extraction). Unlike say a consumer product or durable, that night when a hotel room lay empty or that flight which took off only half-full are not going to come back. Sterling therefore realised that if they were able to predict the number of 'empty' beds, they could create a parallel revenue stream. This led to a strategy to build a strong Free Independent Traveller (FIT) sales system.

After JRK left Sterling, in came Ramesh Ramanathan, yet another marketing veteran. In our first meeting itself I discovered that we shared an alma mater (Indian Institute of Management, Calcutta; incidentally so did JRK). And to my relief I also realised that Ramesh wanted to continue using the services of our agency for the FIT marketing efforts, though he was planning to change the ad agency handling the time share advertising account.

In the service industry you get to meet a wide variety of clients and not all of them are the same. Some like to hear the sound of their own voice. Some are monosyllabic. Some wax eloquent about everything under the sun. Some are keen listeners. Some give you industry gossip. Some look for industry gossip from you. Some ask your opinion about things that are unconnected with you. Some don't let you step out of line, even by an inch. Some challenge everything you present, often to agree in the end. Some accept everything you present, a scary proposition, putting tremendous pressure on you never to recommend something that is even remotely doubtful.

In Ramesh, I discovered a person who loved books. I realised, early in our chats, that he was a voracious reader and loved to learn from books and apply them to business.

In one such meeting Ramesh spoke gloriously about a new book he had read. He mentioned the name of the book, the author and the principles elucidated in the book. The book spoke about the importance of training front-line sales and service staff in the hospitality and tourism industry and how they had to be empowered to take decisions that could satisfy the customer. No service manual can cover all the various situations that may be encountered by frontline staff. So unless they imbibe the concept of customer service, at all times, they will falter, was the contention of the book.

Ramesh explained how he was trying to apply the principles of the book to Sterling's resort operations. You get all kinds of customers, he opined. Some want to cook (time share holiday resorts offer kitchenette facilities), but some want to dine out. Some have small kids whom they obsess over, some want to leave their kids at the play booth. Some bring their elderly parents along. Some come with extended families. Some have severe diet restrictions. Some are habitual complainers. Some are in awe of the resort staff. And so on.

The variation is endless, Ramesh explained. So unless the staff internalise the ethos of 'caring for the customer', the operation would fall flat. It is also likely that the same customers would visit the following year. And if they did not have a good experience, they would stop coming, and more importantly share their negative experience. As they say in marketing, a satisfied customer will speak about his experience with two people. A dissatisfied customer will speak to twenty about his lousy experience (this was before social media; now multiply that by a factor of ten).

I left Ramesh's room making a mental note that I should buy the book he had spoken about so eloquently. But soon enough I forgot the name of the book (it was many years later that I adopted the habit of carrying a little black notebook at all times, something that my friends make fun of).

A few weeks later I was at the Landmark book store and as was my habit, after reviewing the front section for the latest arrivals and best sellers, I moved to the management section. I then recalled that Ramesh had spoken to me about this book on exceptional customer service. But for the life of me, I could not remember the name of the book. As I approached a sales assistant, I realised that I had forgotten the name of the author as well. All I remembered was that it was a book on customer service. And it was written by the CEO of an airline.

The poor sales assistant gave up and asked me to recall some more details. And though I tried hard (this was before the age of mobiles; today, the same problem could have been solved with a quick text message to Ramesh; but stay with me on this story, it has an interesting twist), I could not remember the name of the book or the name of the author.

Seeing me in deep conversation with a rather harassed sales assistant in the shop, the promoter of Landmark book stores, Ms Hemu Ramaiah, who was in the store, approached us. She asked the assistant why he was not able to find the book. I intervened and told her that it was totally my fault. I did not remember the book's title or the author's name. She asked me what the book was about. I explained that the book was about exceptional customer service and it was a thin book. She wanted to know if I knew any other details about the book. I said that the book was written by the CEO of an airline. 'I think the airline is SAS (Scandinavian Airline System)', I murmured.

'Oh, oh. Yes, I think I know the book!' Hemu exclaimed. 'We have it and let us look for it once again.' And sure as hell we found the book a few minutes later. The book: *Moment of Truth*, the author: Jan Carlzon.

The moment we found the book, Hemu asked the sales assistant how he did not know that Landmark had the book. He smiled sheepishly. I was amazed that Hemu remembered that they had the book and asked her if she read all the books in her large bookstore. She explained that it was the responsibility of the store assistant to know every book that was in the section he was looking after. They need not read the whole book, but should have read at least the front and back cover of the book. Yes, the book's cover did explain what the book was about and the fact that Jan Carlzon was the CEO of SAS.

I was amazed at how we could find a particular book, without the name and the author's name, all in less than ten minutes. I wonder if this experiment can be repeated in any book store in the world (Amazon and Flipkart excluded). I suspect the rise of independent book stores has a lot to do with this kind of love for books. The book seller and the book buyer are kindred spirits. Their love for books transcends the mere commercial transaction that takes place.

A week later, I told Ramesh that I had managed to get hold of the book and had finished reading it. I also narrated the story of my book purchase. And we both agreed that this story in itself was an example of the ethos of the 'Moment of Truth' idea.

The book was based on the premise that every sales or service person in an airline, or any other industry, who is in a customer-facing situation, gets to face peculiar challenges all the time. Those moments are 'moments of truth'. If the employee is able to rise to the challenge of that moment, he wins the everlasting love and loyalty of the customer.

In the book, Jan Carlzon narrates the story of an SAS business customer checking in at the Stockholm airport. As the customer takes out his tickets, he realises that he has the ticket, but not his passport. As he panics, the calm counter clerk asks him where he may have left the passport. The customer remembers leaving the passport on the table in the room at a city hotel. The counter staff requests the customer to take a seat and tells him that he will take the flight as planned.

Now comes the going-the-extra-mile story, almost literally. The counter staff then calls the hotel and tells them the story. The hotel confirms that the passport is with their reception staff. They had held on to it hoping that the guest would come back. The airline staff then requests the hotel to send the passport through a mobike courier and confirms that the cost of $25 would be paid by the airline. The passport reaches the airport in thirty minutes. And the passenger, delighted, boards the flight, just in time.

Did the counter staff have to ask her superior before she spent the $25? No! Did she have to get approval from someone before extending this helping arm? No!

Jan Carlzon explains in the book that how empowered employees will rise to any challenge that a customer throws at them. And unless they rise to the 'Moment of Truth' challenge, a company's customer service would be patchy, at best.

Thanks to Ramesh, I had discovered a very useful book. And we could have a discussion around the book.

In my long career I have had the good fortune of having many clients suggesting books that I should read.

Chandu Mishra of ITC once told me to read *On War* by Carl Von Clausewitz. And surprised me by saying that he never reads fiction!

R. Gopalakrishnan, the former Director of Tata Sons, a book lover and author of several best-selling books himself is also a constant source of new book information.

Harish Bhat of the Tata Group is yet another avid book lover, author and a great source for new book titles (his columns in the *Hindu Business Line* often refer to books he has recently read).

Building on the work of Carl Jung who presented the concept of archetypes, in the book *The Hero & The Outlaw*, brand strategist Margaret Mark and psychologist Carol Pearsons present twelve archetypes in simple everyday language: Innocent, Regular

Guy, Hero, Outlaw, Explorer, Creator, Ruler, Magician, Lover, Caregiver, Jester and Sage.

A 'Hero' archetype is someone who is willing to brave it out, fight the demons and protect the damsel in distress.

The 'Outlaw' archetype is someone who is ready to break the law to get to his goals.

And a 'Sage' is a wise man, or woman, who is worldly-wise and a constant source of mind-expanding counsel.

The archetype methodology of understanding brands has been widely used. In consumer research we often get consumers to visualise brands (what is the archetype that best suits Nike or Apple or Royal Enfield, etc.).

I believe you can also classify clients into various archetypes. And you may actually be lucky to get a 'Sage' client. If you do, make sure to listen to what they say. You never know, there may be a 'Moment of Truth' experience waiting for you there.

After Action Report

When any Indian service firm like an ad agency ties up with or sells equity to a foreign company, the first thing they hope for is new business. They hope the international arm will just pour new business into the Indian entity. In my experience, this does not happen because the Indian arms of multinationals have reasons to stay with their current local advertising partners. That the parent company is with a certain agency often makes little difference to its Indian counterpart. It does not mean that the Indian arm will shift to that agency's Indian partner/subsidiary. There is a huge amount of inertia and a preference for the status quo. Where the international tie-up helps is if the global agency has a client who is thinking of entering India and so has no local relationships.

So we were delighted to hear from the Austrian arm of our parent agency that their client, who made an energy drink was thinking of entering India. They wanted to know if we were interested and if we had any conflicts and concerns. We did not have any conflicts and told the Austrian agency that we would give the client a warm welcome when they came to visit us in Mumbai.

A few days later, in walked the Austrian client and with him was the Indian CEO of the company, Mr Ani Mohandas. We shared with them the credentials of our agency and the work we had done in the consumer products space. As the meeting ended we shook hands and Ani told us he would meet us for a detailed discussion the following week.

The next meeting with Ani went on for a few hours. We discovered that he had served in the Indian Army and had seen action in Sri Lanka as a part of the IPKF (Indian Peace Keeping Force). He had been injured in action, fractured many bones and had been airlifted from Sri Lanka and recuperated for several months in an army hospital in Bangalore. But nothing of this experience showed on his face. He was a terrific story teller and the hours just flew by. I had not had too many ex-army men as a client and I was happy to hear all his stories, both from his corporate experiences and from his army days.

Ani had a plan on how to grow the business. He wanted to know if he could use our office for occasional meetings, to which we readily agreed. He felt the Austrian parent company did not have a clear picture of the Indian market and we needed to work with Ani to build a template on how to open the market for the brand. They were a late entrant since Red Bull had a head start in the country. And for our work, Ani was willing to pay a fair fee.

As the brand got launched we realised that Ani's idea of selling an energy drink was very different from what we had imagined. He felt the brand could be built by focusing solely on the 'Bar and Restaurant' segment. He was very successful in placing the product in all the bars of Mumbai and wanted us to join him one evening for a market visit.

One fine Friday evening, my colleagues Kinjal Medh and Nitin Karkare met with Ani at the Library Bar in The Taj President hotel in Cuffe Parade. I sipped on a diet cola since I was recovering from a severe attack of jaundice. Ani announced that he was going to take the agency team on the wildest market visit ever. I smiled, knowing I would be dropping off after the first leg or should I say, peg.

I heard the full story, like an After Action Report the next Monday morning. I was told the market visit had started at 8 p.m. at Colaba and went on for more than six hours, all the way to Andheri and back to Bandra. Kinjal felt he had lost count after the first five stops. Nitin remembered at least eight. I asked the brave heroes, why did they have to drink at all the stops? Apparently, Ani charmed them into participating and it came out that at each venue there were people Ani was meeting and doing business with. All they really remembered was being dropped at their respective homes in the wee hours of the morning.

In the service industry we get to meet and learn from a variety of people. And if ex-army folks are an interesting breed, Ani Mohandas is the cherry on the cake. The business continued and Ani had proved to the agency that he was running the business with very little ad support and he could sustain it for a long, long time.

We lost touch till the 26/11 Mumbai attacks happened. He called a day or two day later to ask about the health of the agency folks and if anyone had been caught at the Taj or the Trident. Then he told me yet another story.

Apparently, his Austrian boss had been visiting India during that week and had checked into the Taj Mahal Palace Hotel at Colaba. Ani, as was his wont, had picked him up in the early evening and taken him on the famous 'Ani Bar Tour' of Mumbai. As they hit the second bar in the suburbs, they came to hear of the attack on the Taj Hotel. Ani's boss went into shock. Ani explained that this was a bad attack but Mumbai had seen worse. Ani told him that he should check into another hotel and wait for the situation to clear up. As some readers would remember, it took the army a couple of days to clear the Taj of the terrorists (more on that a little later).

Ani suggested Taj Lands End, the Taj property at Bandra as a possible hotel for the boss. The boss asked if it was near the sea and when Ani confirmed that it was, suggested that Ani find a hotel far from the sea. The terrorists had come by boat and so the boss was not taking chances. The following night Ani met the boss over a drink and the boss realised that he had not told his mom that he was safe. So in front of Ani he called his mom and this is the conversation that Ani overheard:

'Hi, Mom! This is Martin* here.'

'Martin, is that really you? Can't be.'

'Why Mom, I am calling you. It is me.'

'No, it can't be you. I am seeing your photograph on TV and they say you are dead.'

'No, Mom, I am alive. I am speaking with you, right?'

'But they say you are dead. How come?'

The boss man then went on to explain that he had left the Taj Mahal Palace Hotel before the attack, but had not touched base with the Austrian Embassy to confirm he was safe and so the authorities had assumed that he was missing and probably dead. This conversation was as macabre as it may sound and had us in splits when we heard it many days later.

I asked Ani, 'Tell me Ani, you are an army veteran, why did it take so many days to secure the two hotels?' And he had a powerful argument.

He replied, 'I think the army and the special commando force were told by the hotel people that they didn't know how many senior people and international guests were still in the hotel rooms and so were requested not to fire unless fired upon. The army didn't want to kill a guest, Indian or foreign.'

As you would recall, while the commando forces took what appeared to be an exceptionally long time to secure the two hotels, there was no collateral damage. As Ani explained, 'A four-storey

---

* Name changed to protect privacy.

building can be secured in an hour, if we are allowed to shoot on sight. But with the Taj and Trident, I am sure they were not sure who was looking out of the hotel room. It could have been Martin.'

Everyone in the agency loved Ani and his *joie de vivre*. While he was never a large client in monetary terms, he was a big favourite with all of us. And this brings me to the point that I wanted to make.

There are many talented people in the Indian defence forces— Army, Navy and Air Force. Quite a few of them have managed to make a smooth transition to the corporate world.

In my days selling Yellow Pages, our Kolkata colleague was Wing Commander Chowdary, a dynamite of a man who set up a sales team of over 200 sales executives in just two months. Apparently, he got them all marching into office every morning at 9 a.m., army style. They would then fan out all over the city on sales visits.

Then there is Group Captain Vijay Kumar, a friend whose father was a school buddy of my dad. He is the Executive Director of Madras Management Association (MMA) and under his leadership, the MMA has been awarded the best management association in India for seven years running as of 2017. He has been the driving force in the setting up of the MMA Management Centre in the heart of Chennai.

It is said that originally, Harvard Business School set up the Advanced Management Program (AMP), their flagship twelve-week (now eight-week) residential programme for senior managers, for returning World War II officers. These veterans completed the AMP and went on to work in large corporates in the USA. Interestingly, Harvard continues to have strong links with the US Army and Marine Corps. They regularly nominate their high potential officers for the flagship programmes and Harvard often invites senior generals to speak to students. In many strategy classes, there are stories that refer to the US Marines and Army. Some of those are absolutely fascinating. For instance, the concept of the After Action Report (AAR) is something that should be adopted in corporate operations. Just as after each action the US Marines are expected to submit an AAR, it is a good idea to put down an AAR after each new business pitch, win or lose.

In the book *Mavericks at Work*, William C. Taylor and Polly Labarre point out the way to win is to stand out from the crowd and stand for something original. Mavericks manage to win big in business by rethinking the logic of how business gets done, starting from how strategy is made, how ideas are unleashed, how connections are made to consumers, and how to enable the best people to do their best.

I believe that in the suited-booted world of senior management, someone like Ani Mohandas is a maverick. He can change the status quo by taking tough stands and asking a lot of hard questions, army style!

In using army talent in industry and entrepreneurial ventures, no country comes close to what has been achieved by Israel. The book *Start-Up Nation: The Story of Israel's Economic Miracle*, by Dan Senor and Saul Singer identifies the key pillars of that country's start-up magic. The authors identify immigration, research and development and, what may be a surprise to many of you (it was to me), the compulsory military service as the factors that made Israel the start-up champion that it has become. Israel has not only implemented the military service regimen for all youngsters, it has also taken the trouble to identify the brightest of the youngsters and put them in elite tech divisions such as Israeli Defence Forces' 8200 Group. These youngsters then go into sterling careers when they finish their army service. Some go on to do higher studies in highly respected Israeli universities and yes, many of them end up with their own start-ups.

I think if we see more and more ex-service people in the Indian start-up and corporate world we might see some fresh churning of concepts and strategies. Right now, we have a sprinkling of ex-service people in positions like administration and human resources. But I think getting them into operational positions can provide Indian corporates a great new window into how to work and how to get work done. In my career in marketing and advertising I have not met too many ex-Indian Army veterans in operational positions. Ani was an exception.

I wonder if we had more of them, how many new companies may have been born and how many wild market visits I would have been taken on.

Flying Without a Net

GlaxoSmithKline (GSK) is one of India's most respected pharmaceutical companies and when we were invited to pitch to them, we were naturally delighted. The team that had invited us consisted of Mr K. N. Chandrashekar (KNC) and Mr Ashok Bhattacharya. The assignment looked simple enough. GSK had an old multivitamin brand called Cobadex and they now wished to launch a new variant of this brand that would contain antioxidants, in addition to the vitamins that the original product contained. The client was happy to share a lot of information including sales numbers, prescription data, doctor research and a whole lot of other facts and figures. The team from the agency— Gauri Chaudhuri and Kinjal Medh—had a fair bit of experience working on pharmaceutical brands and they crunched their way through all the data given by the client. The ensuing strategy discussions in the agency office also threw up some very different ways to address the new brand opportunity.

The problem, according to the analysis done by the agency's planning team, was that Cobadex was an old brand, a brand that was a habit with a significant number of doctors. Also, anti-oxidants had entered India a decade ago and were no longer news. There were probably a hundred brands offering antioxidants. And all these brands were being promoted vigorously to doctors with product detailing, free samples and gifts. In this clutter there was very little chance that Cobadex's new offering would be remembered.

The new avatar of Cobadex was to be called Cobadex CZS (C standing for Chromium, Z for Zinc and S for Selenium). We wondered if there was a way to market this new offering differently.

In marketing, we are taught that the three key pillars are 'Segmentation', 'Targeting' and 'Positioning'. What if Cobadex CZS segmented the market differently and a niche set of indications were targeted? The brand could then be positioned for that indication. This idea took hold of us.

The idea and the strategy that emerged was to go after the diabetics market since CZS had a very beneficial effect when offered along with other serious diabetic medications. We unearthed some very interesting research and were all set to sell the strategy to the client. There was, however, one big risk in what we wanted to recommend to the company. We wanted to focus the entire sales story on diabetes and not even mention the multi-vitamin ingredients of the brand. Nevertheless, we went ahead.

The presentation to KNC and Ashok Bhattacharya went off well. They appreciated the work done by the agency and the STP (Segmentation-Targeting-Positioning) approach suggested. But they had a serious disagreement with us on the need to drop any reference to the brand's other multivitamin ingredients. They felt that since Cobadex was a multivitamin, how could one talk about it to doctors without speaking about the various vitamins that were in the brand. Our argument was that the doctor knew about Cobadex and what it contained. They didn't need yet another reminder about the vitamins in the brand. The more we spoke about those vitamins, the more we would get grouped with the hundred-plus run-of-the-mill multivitamin brands that also offer antioxidant ingredients. We wanted to positon Cobadex CZS as a very serious brand that could be of help in managing diabetes. The argument raged on for a few days. Finally KNC suggested that we take this divergence of views to the MD of the company, Mr Kal Sundaram.

The meeting with Kal Sundaram was a big surprise to all of us. After hearing the agency's views, he asked the GSK team to voice their concerns. He then outlined the challenges that he saw with the promotion strategy. One issue he highlighted was that GSK medical representatives were quite unused to speaking about diabetes. He saw this as a problem and an opportunity, since globally, GSK was planning to enter the diabetes medication arena in a year or so. Finally, he decided to go with what the agency had suggested. And he thanked us for standing by our convictions.

The agency team walked out of the meeting feeling ten feet tall. But there were many lessons for us in this story. For one, the marketing team at GSK did not shoot down a suggestion which they did not agree with. They questioned the logic and they tested the conviction of the agency, but were willing to take it to their boss. They realised that it was a risky decision and wanted their boss to give his perspective on the decision. I also realised that the MD of a large company like GSK could take the time to sit and discuss the positioning and promotional strategy of a small brand. He too was open to suggestions and was ready to take a leap into new territory. I thought the MD had managed to bring a new perspective to the discussion on the need for the GSK medical rep to understand a new disease process and treatment.

Finally, the brand got launched and to our pleasant surprise, became the largest prescribed antioxidant brand in the Indian market. The teams had moved on, the agency had moved on, but as I read the MD's statement in the GSK annual report, almost seven years after that memorable episode, I noticed that Cobadex CZS continued to be the biggest prescribed antioxidant in India. This happened because the team at GSK was willing to 'fly without a net' as Prof. Thomas J. DeLong would say. When a manager 'flies without a net', he is abandoning his old fears and is ready to take a risk.

That was not the only instance where a client decided to listen to the agency and go against their own instincts about a branding decision. When Tata Motors was planning to launch the sedan version of their successful Indica hatchback car in 2002, the initial idea was to call the car Indica Sedan. Here again, the agency team and client team consisting of Mr Rajiv Dube and Mr S. Krishnan discussed the pros and cons of such a decision. Given the fact that car buying in India was a status decision and a sedan was seen as a higher status car than a hatchback, the agency team was convinced that they needed a different name. Indica, the agency team felt, would not do.

The client team was, however, convinced that the sedan had been built on the same platform as the Indica and shared most of its parts with its smaller sibling, and the name needed to reflect that fact. Finally, however, the team decided to go with a brand name that sounded like Indica but was significantly different, and the Tata Indigo was born. It went on to become India's largest-selling sedan brand and a very profitable brand too. Here again, the point I would like to make is that the client showed a great deal of respect for the agency's point of view. That in itself was a learning.

Jumping to yet another example of a similar situation: Knoll Pharmaceuticals (formerly Boots Company) called us to examine how to take their antacid brand, Digene, from prescription to

OTC.* The trigger was that Gelusil had gone OTC the previous year and a strategy consultant had suggested that Knoll should take Digene OTC in order not to miss the new OTC boom. After looking at all the numbers, the agency team was convinced that Digene should stay as an ethically promoted brand. There were many arguments in favour of this. For one, the company had sold all its hard-core OTC brands (Coldarin, Burnol) and had disbanded its OTC division. So the company did not have those competencies any longer. A simple analysis of media costs showed that a brand like Digene would not benefit from a huge increase in sales in the short term. If the company persisted with heavy advertising for five years, only in the sixth year would the brand be able to recoup the advertising investments and not before that. (In today's terms of cash burn, five years seems short, but in the late '90s companies were wary of such long-term brand investments in advertising.)

We recommended that the brand stay ethical but continue to promote its key attributes to doctors and not leave it entirely to their memory. The team on the client side—Mr Sudarshan Jain and Mr Vineet Kalia—were not convinced to start with. They asked a number of penetrating questions, which led us to building numerous scenarios. Finally, they agreed to the views we had put forth. These were shared with the strategy consultant, who agreed. The path ended up being the right one for Digene. It continued to stay ethical (promoted to doctors) for almost ten years before it went OTC and in the intervening period it probably delivered better margins and contribution to the company than their rival, who had gone OTC much earlier.

---

* Over-the-counter (OTC) drugs are medicines sold directly to a consumer without a prescription from a doctor, as opposed to prescription drugs, which may only be sold to consumers possessing a valid prescription.

Here again what came alive to me was the readiness of the client to listen to a very different view from the partner firm. It was possible that they may have gone the other way, but the fact that they listened was in fact, proof enough.

What happens when we see this in practice? The agency or partner team realises that the client is going to take them seriously. So the team cannot make a recommendation without doing enough due diligence. You cannot go to a client unless you have done sufficient number crunching, consumer work and consumer insight mining. It is your neck on the line, more than ever before. This kind of trust puts a huge onus on the partner agency to work that much harder to deliver.

What does it take for such high achieving managers to listen to a contrarian view? Is it easy? What are the hurdles?

In the fascinating article 'The Paradox of Excellence', published in *Harvard Business Review* (June 2011), Thomas J. Delong and Sara Delong point out that high achievers often undermine their leadership by being afraid to show their own limitations. The high achievers' graph of performance always follows the high performance curve by being focused on results, doing the right things, being highly motivated, craving positive feedback, displaying passion, etc. They point out that high achievers hate to do the right thing poorly, instead, they prefer doing something well, even if it is not the best use of their time. To play the game at a new level or in a new direction calls for humility, it takes practice and patience. That will take them on to the road to doing the right thing well.

In his book *Flying Without a Net*, Prof. Thomas J. Delong expands on what he calls the 'high achievers' trap'. High achievers suffer from anxiety and the fear of being wrong. So they adopt behaviours to relieve the anxiety by being busy and blaming others for their frustrations. However, they need to seek a behaviour that would adapt to gain strength from vulnerability, to put their past behind them and seek new honest feedback.

It is difficult for organisations to look at things differently. In his book *Learning in Action*, Prof. David A. Garwin puts down some guidelines to help organisations learn at work. He asks some simple questions: Does the organisation have a defined learning agenda? Does it learn through experiments, simulations, research, post-audits, benchmarking visits, rather than class room training? Does the organisation accept discordant views and information? Does the organisation avoid repeated mistakes? (The CEO of BancOne John McCoy is reported to have observed, 'I don't remember my successes. It's the mistakes that I learned from.'). Does the organisation lose critical knowledge when people leave? And does the organisation act on what it knows?

In the three stories narrated above, we see high-achieving managers ready to put their anxiety behind them and open up to a fresh way of looking at a problem. They are willing to accept discordant views, something Prof. Garwin insists is a must-do for a learning organisation. By opening up their own thinking to new approaches, they managed to get on to the road of doing the right thing well.

In business, many of the smart people we meet are our vendors, partners and service providers. Are we open to suggestions which may be contrary to what we believe to be true? Instead of rejecting the suggestions, what should we do? Should we ask for more data? Should we ask for proof of concept? In the above examples, the agency was asked to stand up and defend its views. Subsequently, the 'smart people' on the client's side were willing to listen to the agency. They were willing to play a game different from their own—fly without a net, so to speak.

If we can all learn to fly without a net, the sky is the limit, no?

Doing Good. Fairly.

There is a common misconception that people who work for a not-for-profit organisation should all work for free. Or at best, for bare minimum wages. That this is a fallacy on many fronts was a lesson I learnt many years ago.

Bal Mundkur, the founder of Ulka Advertising, spent time in the Indian Navy before getting into the less exciting, or at least less life-threatening world of advertising. He called me one morning to tell me that an old buddy from his Navy days called Rallia Ram had taken over as the CEO of a charity organisation called World Vision located in the city I was based in.

I called the landline number given to me and instantly recognised the voice as that of the same Mr Rallia Ram who had been my client some years earlier. We planned to meet over lunch to figure out how I could be of help to him.

The next week I was at his office and when Mr Ram saw me he remembered the days when I was a young Account Executive handling the ICIM (also known as ICL) computer account. We spoke about the good campaign we had worked on together and a very important exhibition that we helped mount for the company.

Mr Ram had since retired from ICIM and had joined World Vision as their India Head. He then started to explain to me how

World Vision was a charity organisation that got its funding from international sources and now wanted to test if they could increase their domestic fundraising. In this context, he wanted me to examine their fundraising ad campaigns.

We then got out of his office and he had a chauffeur-driven Contessa car waiting for him (those were the days before Indian roads had been invaded by premium brands like Mercedes, BMW, Audi and Jaguar). We went to a fancy restaurant for a hearty lunch. I suppose Mr Ram realised that I was piqued by his lifestyle. Here he was, working in a not-for-profit organisation, but with a fancy car, and was entertaining his agency in a good restaurant. I did not ask, but he decided to broach the topic of executive compensation in the non-profit sector himself.

Mr Ram explained that the prevalent belief among many was that NGOs (non-governmental organisations) and non-profit organisations should employ people who are driven by a larger cause. Hence these organisations should pay their employees wages that are way below what they could earn in the market. He explained that non-profit organisations that paid poor wages ended up losing a lot of the funds in 'leakages'. World Vision was involved in numerous projects and one of their biggest and most unique projects was the 'Adopt a Child' initiative. In this programme, you could undertake to pay a scholarship to a child living in poverty. The programme ensured that the sponsor got a photograph every few months from the child and even an occasional letter. Mr Ram then went on to explain that his organisation had to pay a fair wage to ensure that the money that is supposed to reach the poor actually ends up reaching them.

I did not know that there were clear global norms on how much a charitable organisation should spend on its own management, or what is known as administrative expenses. And the amount is substantial, especially if the organisation has a large field set up, and can be as high as 20 to 30 per cent of the funds being deployed.

I thanked Mr Ram for the lunch (he insisted on paying) and the agency worked on several fundraising ads for World Vision. We discovered that their simple call-for-action ads drew a better response in women-oriented magazines. There were many other such learnings that came our way as we worked with the charity organisation. They insisted on paying us our full commission on all the media we bought and did not spend a minute arguing with us about our rates. We on our part waived our creative and artwork fees; but not because they asked for it.

Mr Ram was just one successful corporate executive who had reinvented his career moving to the NGO sector. I am sure his overall salary package was nowhere in the same league as what he was getting at the British multinational, ICIM. But I saw a man contented with what he was doing. And the lunch with him was a memorable one.

While Mr Ram took over the reins of a successful global NGO, I met yet another corporate CEO who had moved to the other side to create a unique service. This was emergency service operator—108—who wanted to know if they needed to advertise.

The head of operations, Mr Changavali Venkat, an IIM Ahmedabad alumnus and a veteran in the flavours and perfumes industry and as it turned out, someone with whom I had a lot of friends in common. Venkat wanted me to visit his operations centre in Hyderabad and also brainstorm with him on what advertising could do for his service.

Venkat had a very successful career and was known in the perfumery circles as a 'Guru'. I was curious to know what made Venkat move to the non-profit sector. He had an interesting story to tell. Through happenstance he and Mr Ramalinga Raju of Satyam happened to be on the same panel at a conference. They got talking and Mr Raju explained the vision he had for creating a technology-powered emergency response service in Andhra Pradesh. Venkat, a native of Hyderabad was hooked. He decided to move to Hyderabad to help set up the 108 service.

As I toured his facility, he explained that his was a one-of-a-kind service in the world. The 108 ambulances were geographically placed in such a way that they could respond to an emergency call from anywhere in Andhra Pradesh, in sixty minutes or less. They had special permission from the state government to attend to accident victims. Their central monitoring station had doctors on call who could advise the person who called on what first aid could be given. As I spent a few hours in the Central Monitoring Station, I could listen in to some of the conversations and was amazed at the speed at which things were happening. Each modern ambulance was equipped with the latest emergency medical equipment. Venkat explained that each of them even carried metal cutting equipment, since in an automobile accident, it may be required to cut through sheets of metal. The entire 108 operation was the brainchild of Mr Raju, who had supported it financially from Day one.

Venkat got emotional when he explained how they had once got a call from a village and this person said that their neighbour had given birth to a baby girl the previous week and he suspected that they had buried the child alive that morning. The emergency team from 108 was actually able to save the child.

The team at 108, as the team at World Vision, were paid well. But more than that, they were on a mission to respond to emergencies. Apparently they refused to accept any kind of 'tip' from the victim or their family. Also, the service was totally free. Yet another unique feature.

The 108 service combined several unique features, including a state-of-the-art mobile messaging system, mapping and GPS based navigation for the ambulances, hi-tech vans and most importantly, a team of highly committed individuals.

When Satyam went through its share of troubles, I had written in a business newspaper that I hoped that 108 survives the mess. And luckily it did.

How to see hope when you see despair all around is the theme of Viktor E. Frankl's book *Man's Search for Meaning*. It is a must-read book and a classic tribute to hope from a holocaust survivor. In the book he writes, 'Don't aim at success—the more you aim at it and make it a target, the more you are going to miss it. For success like happiness, cannot be pursued; it must ensure and it only does so as the unintended side-effect of one's dedication to a cause greater than oneself or as the by-product of one's surrender to a person other than oneself. Happiness must happen and the same holds for success; you have to let it happen by not caring for it.'

Those were the words going through my mind as I was driving from the 108 head office to the airport. I convinced Venkat that he did not need any advertising and his work was enough to take the brand forward. As I had predicted, 108 was invited by several Chief Ministers, including Gujarat, where the then-CM, Mr Narendra Modi wanted them to start operations as soon as possible, clearing all the red tape in a day.

Coming to the topic of paying a fair wage to people in the NGO sector, I happened to read a wonderful post by Luis Miranda in the Forbes India Blog on 'Challenging the Norms of NGOs'. Luis Miranda is a financial wizard who has worked with the best names in Indian finance before moving to the non-profit sector. In his blog post, he quotes from the book *Give Smart—Philanthropy that Gets Results*, by Thomas J. Tierney (the co-founder of the Bridgespan Group) and Joel L. Fleishman. The authors indicate that one of the traps in the non-profit sector is 'nonprofit neglect'—

the 'widespread resistance to providing general operating support, which grantees can use to develop their organisational capacity'. As a result, NGOs cannot spend scarce resources on bringing in more professional advice or resources. Nor can they spend on proper training and facilities ... because donors don't like funding these things, probably, and they consider them a waste. This in turn has certain consequences, which might not be very good for the organisation.

Given this situation, more and more highly qualified professional CEOs transitioning to the NGO sector is the best news that one can hope for. But as Tierney and Fleishman say, donors need to cut them some slack and help them build organisational capabilities. Like what was done at 108.

Who Reads
Body Copy?

Anyone who has worked in advertising would have heard the question, 'Who ever reads the body copy of the ad? Why are you guys agonising over it?' This story has a twist. It is not just about a client who not only believed that readers of newspapers read body copy, but also took it upon himself to craft it in his own impeccable style.

The legendary American copywriter, the late Howard Luck Gossage, frequently referred to as 'the Socrates of San Francisco', was an advertising innovator and iconoclast during the 'Mad Men' era (the '60s). He is known for having said, 'The object of your advertising should not be to communicate with your consumers or your prospects at all but to terrorise your competition's copywriters.' He is also reported to have written: 'Nobody reads ads. People read what interests them. Sometimes it's an ad.'

The challenge for a copywriter is often to make a subject interesting in the belief that once it is made interesting, a reader will read it.

As a young advertising executive, in the early '80s, I was tasked with handling some of the more challenging or should I say, boring accounts of the agency. One of them was a relatively unknown chemical equipment manufacturer based in Pune. Those were the days before the Mumbai-Pune Expressway had come into existence. One had to make one's way to the Bombay-Pune taxi stand in Dadar to grab a share taxi. Then a taxi ride with total strangers for four hours. Post that, a meeting at the client's factory in Chinchwad, a Pune suburb that could take five hours. Then hop on to a share taxi for the ride back. It was a tough job, even though the industry went by the glamorous name—'Advertising'.

I was a little lucky with this client. A few months after I started handling the account, the client called us (me and my boss P. S. 'Vish' Viswanathan) for an important meeting. My preparation for this important meeting included asking the senior colleagues what I had to be ready with. Someone suggested that this company, then called Wanson, had briefed the agency on a name change to Thermax. Several meetings on a new logo had already taken place even before I came on to the account. I hoped I would be lucky and one of the logos designed would be accepted.

The meeting turned out to be a lot more interesting than we had imagined. Yes, the company was changing its name to Thermax. Yes, they needed a new logo. And the team instantly approved one of the shortlisted logos (the agency team back in Mumbai refused to believe that this had really happened so fast).

The MD of the company, Mr R. D. Aga was chairing the meeting himself and he wanted to hear what the company should do to ensure that the name change was accepted well.

To answer that, Vish wanted to know what the client thought about their image with their customers and prospects would be like. The team at Wanson was sheepish. They stated that they were not sure. Being an engineer-dominated company, they had not paid any attention to brand, image and other such soft issues.

The agency team then suggested that they should conduct an

image survey. 'What is that?' was the question posed to us. Vish had earlier run Lintas ad agency's marketing research division, I was also a big believer of consumer or user research. So we explained the process and felt that Wanson should survey its own customers and prospects, to see what they thought of the company. Since Wanson was going to be doing customer research for the first time, we decided to approach the then-leading marketing research agency, IMRB. Our meeting with Dorab Sopariwala from IMRB (who, readers may know from his television appearances as a psephologist), went well. Based on Dorab's suggestion we added a few other companies such as Larsen & Toubro, Westerwork, and Siemens to benchmark Wanson's image.

The research presentation took place in the Mumbai office of the agency, and the Wanson team was in for a surprise. They had imagined that their image would come way below that of the companies identified as benchmarks. But their image came out, almost at the top. How could this happen? Well, the truth was that they made a variety of boilers, thermic fluid heaters, heat exchangers, etc. and all the calls they got were complaint calls. They did not interact much with customers otherwise. So their own self-image had taken a beating. It took us a while to convince them that their image was actually way above par and they ought to be proud of what they had been able to achieve.

It was now clear that the Wanson brand image and goodwill had to be transferred to the new name, Thermax. And the new brand Thermax had to be built to take the company forward to the next decade and beyond.

The agency team suggested a simple three ad 'Name Change' campaign, to be followed by a six-ad print campaign on the various product process successes of Thermax (formerly Wanson).

Any good advertising is only as good as the brief. So Vish had asked me to read up all I could about the products, innovations and case studies of Wanson's successes. Based on my extensive reading, I had managed to prepare a brief that was rich in product details. The creative team, the legendary copywriter Kamlesh Pandey and much-awarded art director Arun Kale, worked on the campaign. What they produced were a series of six ads. The dominant visual of the ad was the new Thermax logo, but each ad showcased one unique product. And in a first, each ad also had an inset that gave more technical details about the product.

We did not expect the selling job to be as simple as it turned out. But in one meeting the client team headed by Mr R. D. Aga cleared the name change campaign. Mr Aga questioned me about the six product-based corporate brand image ads. He wanted to know where I had obtained all the information and if the claims made in the headlines were really tenable. Obviously, he knew his facts but was testing my conviction. The fact that I was a chemical engineer by qualification may have helped the selling process, I admit.

As we were leaving the meeting, Mr Aga requested me to give him a complete set of body copy sheets of the six corporate ads. I was not sure why the MD of a large company would want to read body copy. How wrong I was. This MD was not planning to read the body copy. He was planning to write it!

Creating ads for industrial products like lathes, boilers, electrical motors, etc. are at best treated as a chore in an ad agency. Writing body copy for these ads is a double chore. So most agencies leave the writing to junior copywriters.

The copy sheets I had left with Mr Aga had all been crafted not by a junior copywriter, but by Kamlesh Pandey himself.

About a week later a courier package arrived from Pune. I got a call from the Wanson Mumbai office saying that this package was from their MD and I should arrange to have the package picked up ASAP.

As I opened the package, I was not sure of what to expect. Had they changed their mind about the campaign? Did Mr Aga want major changes?

The envelope contained the six copy sheets of the six-ad campaign that I had left with Mr Aga. It also contained a note from Mr Aga saying that he had taken the liberty of recrafting the body copy of the six ads, keeping the concept and headline as it was originally presented.

Writing copy for what is known as a long copy ad is a challenge. It is a bigger challenge if the ad has multiple boxes and visuals. The copy sheets I had left behind had taken care of the word count of the body copy of each ad, as well as the word count of the technical inset case. So I knew that Mr Aga was trying his hand at something quite tricky.

I need not have worried. As I began reading the first ad copy written by Mr Aga, I realised that this was not just copy written by a copywriter but by someone who believed every single word he had written. The copy had the perfect cadence and the technical inset was technical no doubt, but not too technical for the general reader. All six ads had been crafted to perfection by Mr Aga. I realised that Mr Aga, an Oxford English graduate (and a Harvard Business School alumnus) had put his knowledge of both English and Engineering to perfect use.

The ad was read by some of us at the agency and to be honest we had not read such well-written industrial ad copy ever before. Kamlesh Pandey was not amused that we preferred Mr Aga's copy to his. But somehow I managed to use some higher powers to get Kamlesh to agree (to be fair, every ad used the exact headline and sub-heads as created by Kamlesh).

The campaign broke as planned. The ads were widely acclaimed as a breakthrough in industrial product advertising. My father, who knew very little about engineering products commented that he read every word of the six ads (the ads appeared in the leading dailies); that was high praise indeed.

The Ad Club awards for creative excellence chose the Thermax campaign as the Best Corporate Campaign of the Year.

Thermax went on to become one of the most respected industrial product companies in India ... aided, to some degree, by the corporate name change, identity change and the corporate campaign!

As I narrate this tale, I am filled with a sense of awe and respect for Mr R. D. Aga (who passed away at a relatively young age in 1996). He believed in the importance of the ad campaign so much that not only did he sit in on all the meetings, but decided to write the body copy himself. Maybe he realised that he was in fact best qualified to do the job.

The lesson I learnt was that if you are committed enough to a task, you will find the time to do it and do it well. You will not rest till you have got it right.

I remember calling Mr Aga to thank him for the copy and let him know that we would not make any changes in what he had written. He laughed and asked if we were saying that because it was the client's copy. Not at all, was my reply.

Mr Aga probably enjoyed writing and rewriting the copy, polishing it to perfection. As the Hungarian psychologist Mihaly Csikszentmihalyi (pronounced as 'Me High Chick Sent Me High') writes in his book *Flow*, 'Flow is the way people describe their state of mind when consciousness is harmoniously ordered and they want to pursue whatever they are doing for its own sake'. I can almost imagine Mr Aga in a 'flow' state writing the body copy of the six ads. A managing director of an engineering company, finely crafting body copy.

In the article, 'Level 5 Leadership', Prof. Jim Collins (*Harvard Business Review* July–August 2005) writes that Level 5 leaders demonstrate the triumph of humility and fierce resolve. The Level 1 executives show High Capability, they have great skills, knowledge and work habits. Level 2 leaders have a Contributing Team Member approach, they work towards group objectives tirelessly. Level 3 leaders are Competent Managers and they are able to organise people and resources. Level 4 leaders are seen as 'Effective Leaders', they can catalyse commitment towards a vision. The Level 5 leader is beyond all this. They are actually a paradoxical combination of personal humility plus professional will. They are able to set aside their top hat and work with people way below their level on humble tasks.

Working with Mr R. D. Aga on the Thermax campaign taught me some valuable lessons. There is nothing that is too small for a leader who is striving to achieve the best and raise his organisation to perform at a higher level.

To such leaders, even the body copy of an ad matters.

Setting the Right Expectations

We were rather surprised to get a call from Cadbury. It was and continues to be one of the most respected consumer marketing companies. But, they rarely called ad agencies for a pitch or even for a credentials meeting. Also, our agency had handled some of their competing brands for years, or should I say, decades.

But when a client like Cadbury calls, you land up pronto. Old Ad World Saying.

Sanjay Purohit, the Head of Marketing, wanted to meet us to find out something he had heard we had in our kitchen: a secret sauce to figure out competitive strategies. Chandramouli Venkatesan, the Head of Strategy at Cadbury had alerted Sanjay about this magic potion of ours.

The meeting with Sanjay went very well. We took him through the 'Chess' competitive gaming tool that we had developed. In fact, it was a powerful process that had been conceived originally by Foot Cone Belding's account planning team in New York. We in India had continued to use it as a part of the Cogito consulting practice, though its use internationally had waned in the 2000s.

The presentation that was made included the process that was used to unearth competitive strategies (without violating any of the laws of the land, if I may add). The lengthy process usually took anything between two to four months. The client had to identify the two to five competitors they wanted to study. For each of these competitors, we would dig up all published information and then bolster it with some one-on-one interviews. The folks interviewed would be subject matter experts, dealers, consultants, media professionals, financial analysts, etc. All these interviews would be done only by the senior executives of the consulting team, and often it took a day trip to Delhi or Bhopal just to meet with someone for one hour.

The credentials deck of Chess contained some powerful case studies (with sufficient name masking) and those were also shared with Sanjay. After the long presentation, Sanjay, no pushover as far as strategic thinking is concerned, was reasonably impressed. But he had a trick question up his sleeve.

He asked, 'You guys handle some of our competitors in your ad agency business. And you said that to do Chess you need to also study the competitive behaviour of Cadbury. How will I share any confidential information with you? Can the study be done without that crucial piece of data?'

We were thrown by that question, but given that 'Never Say Die' was our guiding credo, we explained that we would work with just the public domain information available on Cadbury. We would not seek any so-called confidential information from them and explained that this would work well.

Sanjay then wanted to get into the details of the process and the meeting went on for another hour.

At the end of the meeting, as we were walking out of the eponymous Cadbury building, we were delighted. This looked like a great project to work on. But a nagging fear remained.

Why is Cadbury asking us to do this project? Was there something we were missing?

In the past we had done Chess projects for leading Indian groups such as Tata, ITC and Forbes Marshall. We had also presented Chess to some of the most respectable MNC FMCG companies in India, who often listened and then threw some MNC rule book at us. In one case, we were told that this would violate their corporate governance norms. We went blue in the face trying to explain we would not violate any norms. The task involved, in large measure, reconfiguring information that was already in the public domain. We were not going to go around snooping and doing skullduggery, shady surveillance or espionage work. If we were speaking to anyone, like a distributor or a former employee, we were duty-bound to tell them what the project was about. So how were we in violation of any rule? Despite these disclaimers, the MNC projects would not move past the first meeting.

Meanwhile, the Cadbury story was moving forward at a breakneck pace. So I sought a meeting with the Managing Director of Cadbury, Anand Kripalu. We had been friends for years though we had never worked together or even as a client–agency. We hailed from the same alma mater twice over, and often had good stories to share.

But this, competitive gaming, was a serious matter.

I decided to ask Anand the 'Why us?' question. My long soliloquy went something like this: 'Anand, we are really delighted that Mouli remembered our Chess process and asked Sanjay to chat with us. Sanjay seems convinced about the power and utility of this unique tool. But I have a serious doubt. You have some of the best talent working with you. Your marketing team is probably the best in the country. Your strategy team is also way above par. We are elated that you chose to work with us. But I want to set our expectations straight. I am not sure if we will discover something that your team would not have spotted if they want about it systematically. I am worried that we could end up coming a cropper. You are a friend and Cadbury is a highly respected company. So I don't want to make tall promises and bite the dust after a few months.'

Anand listened to me carefully and then responded with a lot of candour, 'I perfectly understand what you are saying. We have a great team and we do fabulous work in product development, packaging, marketing, advertising, etc. That is a problem in some sense. I wonder if we are a little too complacent. I think my team should work with your crack strategy team. In that interaction, I am sure my team will learn a few new tricks. Maybe we will discover something that has missed our eagle eyes earlier. Maybe we will not. But either way I am sure something good will come out of this. Not to worry, my friend, let us do this and see what comes out.'

I was relieved to hear this from Anand. He did realise what I was trying to do. I wanted to set expectations at a reasonably low level, so that we were not held guilty after the process, which was costly and time-consuming, was completed.

The next three months were quite exciting for the strategy team. Many trips were made to meet subject matter experts. International calls were made to get deeper insights into the new competitors who were entering India. Our own senior strategy specialists including Dorab Sopariwala, Niteen Bhagwat, Minitha Saxena and Kinjal Medh were pulled neck deep into the project.

Finally, when we assembled all the information we had gathered, we started to see some interesting patterns. We were confident that the project results would pass muster. The competitors whom Cadbury had identified as the biggest threat, we found out, were not the real threat. It was another player. Cadbury had also become predictable in its marketing and innovation game. We had several more such nuggets.

To his credit, Anand decided to have a full day off-site with his top team, representing sales, marketing, strategy, production, supply chain, finance and HR. The presentations and the gaming sessions threw up interesting challenges for Cadbury and some exciting opportunities.

Some years later we were chatting about this project and I casually mentioned how I admired him for taking a chance with us on the project. He turned serious. And said with utmost modesty, 'Ambi, that Chess thing got us thinking afresh. And do you know a Rs 1000 crore product opportunity came out of that? So I am happy that I took that chance and thanks to your team for helping us pull a big rabbit out of the purple hat.' (Purple is the colour of the Cadbury brand.)

I had to be doubly grateful to Anand. Not only was he generous enough to give us the project, but he was also gracious enough to acknowledge that the project had resulted in measurable business results.

In my career, I have been lucky to have had several clients who were willing to take a chance with what was being recommended and later remembered to thank the agency for sticking our neck out. This was a special case since Anand was able to quantify the results so precisely.

In the book *The Tao of Coaching*, the author Max Landsberg speaks of how goals have to be SMART (Specific, Measurable, Actionable, Realistic and Timely). We may have the skill to do something, but do we have the will; and vice versa. Lastly, mentoring has to do with listening, extracting appropriate information, delegating tasks and authority.

Modern organisations need to develop an ability to learn better. In the article 'Why Learning is Central to Sustained Innovation' (*MIT Sloan Management Review*, Spring 2016), Professors Michael Balle and colleagues point out that many managers think they can create better products just by improving the development process or adding new tools. They say that the key is skilled people and not processes that create great products. The three questions that need to be asked are: What do we need to learn about our customers, products, competitors and production processes to design better products? How do we learn what we need to know about standards, creative problem solving and testing methods? What organisational structures and routines will support the learning?

They explain that organisations that create better products continuously invest in developing the skills of their product developers. They think in terms of streams of products and not of developing single products. The also enhance their own learning through standards, testing models and creative problem solving.

I think therein hangs a tale.

The entire Chess exercise was done not for discovering some mystery sword to destroy the competitive dragon. But it was used to help the team at Cadbury to enhance its own ways of looking at the product development process. And it did produce some magical results.

On my part, I realised that I was wise in setting expectations at a very realistic level. And then exceeding it.

Your Tax Dollars At Work

The agency was abuzz with excitement. Of the wrong kind. We heard that the Chief Income Tax (IT) Commissioner of Mumbai wanted to visit the agency.

We were not sure why such a senior member of the Direct Tax department would be interested in visiting an ad agency. He could have easily called us to his office and we would have gone running. But as it turned out I was given the job of standing at the reception and ensuring that no time was wasted in welcoming and taking Mr G. S. Sidhu, the brisk-talking, brisk-walking Chief IT Commissioner to our Chairman's office.

What transpired was an interesting conversation. Mr Sidhu was not interested in looking into our tax records or our income statements. He was keen on understanding if advertising could be of help to the IT Department. Remember this happened in the late '90s.

The discussion went on for an hour or more and we were requested to present our thoughts to the Member, Central Board of Direct Taxes, Mr N. Rangachary the following week, when he was visiting Mumbai.

A week later, the agency team walked into Aayakar Bhavan (the Income Tax Office, near Churchgate railway station, Mumbai). For once we were all dressed in our suits, and were escorted to the big conference room by the officer who was waiting for our arrival at the front entrance reception, at twelve noon.

In the conference room, we met Mr Sidhu and Mr Rangachary (and a number of other senior IT officers in Mumbai). Anil Kapoor, the chief of the agency started asking Mr Rangachary a set of questions. Mr Rangachary explained that paying tax in this country was seen as a sin. No one wanted to pay taxes and among the rich, it was a pastime to brag about the latest tax avoidance technique used by them. Why were we such poor tax payers, was the question that Mr Rangachary was struggling to answer. Is there something that the government of India could or should do? Could advertisng and marketing help?

The discussion that followed was fascinating. Mr Kapoor explained that the common man saw the government as a money-guzzling monster. They felt all that they paid as taxes was just wasted away. And the government had made no effort to explain how our tax money is used. While we complained about the bad roads, we didn't for a moment think about the abysmally low tax compliance in the country. We didn't think for a moment that it was the taxes we pay that would fund the police, law enforcement agencies, the defence forces and so on. He pointed out that internationally, too, there was deep distrust in the tax department and a morbid fear as well. But in many countries tax departments made a special effort to reach out to audiences to explain how their tax money was being used. For example in the United States of America, when a big highway was being constructed, it was not unusual to see signboards saying 'Your Tax Dollars at Work'. Mr Rangachary listened with rapt attention and then said, 'Mr Kapoor, I wish I could make all my thousand-plus income tax commissioners listen to your passionate discourse.'

We were told that it was likely that we would be called to Delhi for a more elaborate meeting. We thought that it was just an empty promise. But we were surprised when we were told that the next week we had to make a formal presentation to the Chief of the Central Board of Direct Taxes. We had to tell the highest tax authorities how they were doing a lousy job of communicating with their stakeholders and what they could do to remedy the situation.

The Finance Ministry and the Central Board of Direct Taxes (CBDT) are housed in the North Block of the Secretariat Complex in Delhi. The South Block houses the Defence Ministry and several other government departments. As we walked into the North Block, we were beginning to wonder what adventure was in store for us. What did Mr Rangachary want from the meeting? Would we live up to those expectations? Would the seniors even want to listen to us pedlars of ads?

What could some advertising professionals teach the wizened men of North Block, we wondered.

We need not have worried. Virtually, the entire CBDT Board sat through our presentation. We spoke about consumer behaviour and the perceptions that cloud all consumer judgements. The examples we gave were from consumer products and services. And we linked the learning from all those successful campaigns to what the IT department faced. A total lack of communication and trust, between the organisation and the tax-paying public.

The questions were incisive and insightful. And the meeting lasted more than two hours, way past the closing hours of the government offices of Delhi. My colleague Arvind Wable and I were quite amazed at the quality of questions we had to face. We explained that changing perceptions was not a short-term task and the IT department would need to work on a long-term plan to make that happen. We offered our services for free, as a goodwill gesture for the betterment of the country.

As we left the North Block that dark night, we were filled with hope. We realised that in the senior echelons of power of the dreaded Income Tax department sat a group of thorough professionals who cared deeply for their country's progress. We realised that they were open to listening to ideas that went absolutely contrary to what they believed about consumer or tax-payer behaviour. What was also amazing was their ability to listen to criticism.

A few weeks later we were requested to create a print campaign that could be run in local papers, glorifying honest tax payers. I still remember that one of the actual people presented in the first set of ads was the 'Muchhad Paanwala' from Breach Candy, Mumbai. The small campaign ended and though I may want to claim otherwise, it did not create any ripples.

Was this all that the IT Dept would do to reach out to citizens, was a genuine fear we had.

This was too little to achieve a change in perception. A year or so later the government of India launched its first Voluntary Disclosure of Income Scheme (VDIS). The scheme was widely advertised and many of the points we had made at the North Block meeting were presented in the campaign that accompanied the VDIS scheme.

In the article headlined, '18 YEARS AGO, A TAX AMNESTY SCHEME THAT WORKED AND WHY', Shaji Vikraman of *Indian Express* (5 April, 2017) said, 'Under the VDIS, irrespective of the year or nature or source of funds, the amount disclosed, either as cash, securities or assets, whether in India or abroad, was to be charged at the highest tax rate. But at 30 per cent acquisition value, many were drawn to the scheme.' He also noted, 'The roadshows and marketing spearheaded by the savvy Singh (N. K. Singh was revenue secretary) worked—the government netted Rs 10,000 crores in taxes alone, which meant that the mobilisation was substantially higher, putting in the shade five other amnesty schemes launched earlier.'

In some small way our presentation in North Block had taught the Income Tax department that they too need to learn to market and communicate better.

In 1997, the government figures showed that there were just 12 million tax assessees and only 12,000 taxpayers whose income topped Rs 10 lakhs (Rs 1 million). The numbers have moved up over the last twenty years, but it is nowhere near what it should be. For a country of 120 crores (1.2 billion) people, only 3.7 crore (37 million) filed tax returns in 2015-16; of these, 99 lakh (9.9 million) showed income below the exemption limit of Rs 2.5 lakhs (Rs 250,000); 1.95 crore (19.5 million) showed income between Rs 2.5 lacs and Rs 5 lakhs (Rs 250,000 to Rs 500,000); 52 lakh (5.2 million) between Rs 5 lakhs and Rs 10 lakhs (Rs 500,000 to Rs 1 million); only 24 lakh (2.4 million) showed income of over Rs 10 lakhs; only 172,000 people declared income exceeding Rs 50 lakhs (Rs 5 million). This is surprising since in the period 2010 to 2015 more than 1.25 crore (12.5 million) cars have been sold and 2 crore (20 million) Indians have travelled abroad.

The moves by the government of India such as demonetisation (executed in November 2017) has netted 91 lakh (9.1 million) new tax payers for the IT Department. There is this debate about the low tax base in India, but the bigger problem may be the low amount of tax paid by the 3.7 crore (37 million) assessees. When asked about this at a public forum, the former Finance Minister P. Chidambaram pointed out to the fact that agricultural income is not taxable as per the Constitution of India. So I was happy to read Niti Aayog Member Bibek Debroy, in his individual capacity, writing about the need to bring agricultural income under some level of scrutiny.

I think some of these actions will happen far sooner than we expect.

Finally, to close out this story, we were indeed honoured to have been invited to present our thoughts to the most senior of all the think tanks at North Block. It was probably the first time that an advertising agency was asked to present tax collection/communication strategies to the highest direct taxation body of the country. It was an eye-opener to realise that not only were they eager listeners but in their own way they understood what we were driving towards and implemented some of those strategies. Maybe a lot more needs to be done, and who knows, maybe another agency is burning the midnight oil for a presentation to CBDT scheduled for tomorrow evening.

Missing the Big
Blue Ocean

It was the first meeting we were having with our new global client, a client who had worked with Foote Cone Belding (FCB)[*] Chicago, for decades, and were in India in a joint venture with Hindustan Unilever. We were having lunch at a nice restaurant in Pune. My then-boss and mentor Anil Kapoor was in full flow. With us were the Regional Director of FCB Asia-Pacific, the Managing Director (MD) of Lever Johnson (the joint-venture company) and the head of marketing of Lever Johnson.

A little background might help. S. C. Johnson (SCJ) is a highly respected packaged goods company located in Racine, a small town that is a two-hour drive from Chicago. The company proudly states that it is still a 'family-managed company' and is currently run by a third-generation Johnson family member. Their head office is an architectural marvel, designed by none

---

[*] Foote Cone Belding (FCB) and Ulka were partners then. Ulka Advertising, which was an Indian agency did an equity tie-up with one of America's biggest agencies, FCB in 1997. FCB Ulka became fully American-owned in 2007.

other than Francis Lloyd Wright (who was also the architect who designed the Guggenheim Museum in New York). They have special tours at their Head Office where a trained guide takes you through the history of the building, not failing to mention how the local authorities did not initially give building permission to the company, fearing that the 'lotus stem' structure of the building would not be able to take the structural weight. The company makes a whole variety of products such as insect control sprays, floor waxes (Johnson's Wax was the first product made by the company), bathroom cleaners, floor cleaners and room fresheners.

At the lunch in Pune, Anil Kapoor questioned the MD about the logic behind the tie-up between two global players who in fact compete in many countries. The MD explained that the company needed the market reach of Hindustan Lever; HLL has India's best distribution system that works like clockwork, supplying hundreds of products (stock keeping units or SKUs in industry parlance) to millions of retail outlets across India. This explanation did not satisfy Anil Kapoor who now asked why Lever Johnson wanted to reach its products to millions of outlets in small town India. Weren't their products (then insect control sprays and air freshener sprays) aimed more at upper-income urban households? Wouldn't the company be better off with a focused field operation? He even went on to explain how it would be possible to set up a crack team of sixty members to handle the portfolio that Lever Johnson had and would have in its armory in the near future. This core group would bring dedication and commitment to the task at hand and the products of the company would get the attention they deserve. The MD was not amused to hear a sermon about better sales strategies from his yet-to-be-appointed Indian agency head.

The conversation was about to take an ugly turn when the Regional Director decided to intervene and speak about life in Pune and the golfing handicap of the MD. This gave the MD a chance to digress. As we left the lunch the marketing head cornered me and asked me who we thought we were, giving sales organisation advice to folks who had virtually invented sales management. I ducked the question and instead asked for a date for our job review meeting to get the show on the road.

I realised that this global client needed to be handled differently. But I did not know we would again be in a similar discussion ... soon!

This time it was a different person asking the questions. FCB Chicago handled the S. C. Johnson account globally, in more than sixty countries. The global management team in FCB Chicago consisted of two wonderful guys, called the Marks Brothers— Mark Pachhini and Mark Modesto. Mark Pachhini was in charge of Asia and South America and made it a habit to visit all the countries on his watch at least once a year. He was also the designated expert on the insect control category, having worked on the brand Raid for well over twenty years.

Mark was in India to review the Lever Johnson business and I was to debrief him. As we were showing Mark the various SKUs of Lever Johnson as well as the competitive products, he paused to ask a few questions when he saw the brand All Out, which was in an innovative liquid vaporiser format. He wanted to know how the brand was doing. Our planning team explained that the brand was from a Delhi-based company and was primarily being promoted on niche TV channels. We felt that it was a fringe player and may remain so for a long time. He disagreed but said he would take it up at the client meeting the following day.

In Pune, the client was delighted to meet Mark, a person who was held in very high regard across the global SCJ system. The marketing team at Lever Johnson presented their two-/three-year plans. They were planning to roll out Raid mosquito mats as well as Raid coils in the next two years, in addition to Raid insect spray.

They explained that mats were the biggest category in the Indian market and coils too were seeing good growth.

Mark then decided to pose the liquid vaporiser (LV) question. What did Lever Johnson think about the new category being pioneered by the brand All Out? Did they have plans to enter the LV category? LV was after all a category where Raid had a big play in many markets.

The client explained that LV was as yet too niche and Lever Johnson was not interested in niches, but wanted to go after the belly of the market, hence mosquito mats and coils. Mark, in his own polite way decided to question this belief. He was firm on the fact that as an innovator, and SCJ was widely known as a very nimble innovative organisation, they needed to take the initiative to create new categories in India as well. And not stick to the tried-and-tested mats and coils. The discussion continued for more than an hour with Mark sticking to his point of view. But finally the client won the battle by saying that the company was keen on growing fast and they could only do that by going with the tide.

To end this story, the company Lever Johnson launched a number of products such as Raid mats, Raid coils and even Glade incense sticks. The idea was that these mass-market products would benefit from the large Lever network of salesmen and dealers.

It was not to be. Eventually, the company decided to shut its Indian operation.

There is an interesting follow-up to this story, though. Almost seven years later, S. C. Johnson decided to enter the country again. This time, they decided to buy a successful Indian brand. Any guess which brand?

It was the very same All Out LV that was the topic of discussion in Pune with Mark Pachhini. The company entered the country once again. K. K. Sridhar (KK), a Hindustan Lever veteran who had moved to S. C. Johnson a decade earlier was instrumental in the acquisition. KK called me to Delhi to put in place a team to handle the account. I was delighted to see this happen. S. C. Johnson managed to complete the transition successfully.

Thinking back about the sequence of events, I wonder at times why the client did not pay heed to what the agency partner was saying.

From the start we had maintained that S. C. Johnson was a company that had expertise in the top-end of the market, not at the bottom-end, something that Hindustan Lever was a champion at. But our point of view and those arguments about having a small dedicated field force had fallen on deaf ears.

Then the meeting with Mark Pachhini. Thinking back, Mark had made a very valid point. The company was well-positioned to launch liquid vaporisers. Instead, they were playing a catch-up game with the market leaders by launching mats and coils, when they could have created their own 'Blue Ocean' in LVs.

I wish Mark, who is a voracious reader, had presented the team with the book *Blue Ocean Strategy* or may be the book hadn't been published then. I am not very sure.

Blue Ocean Strategy is a marketing theory from the book of the same name, published in 2005, written by W. Chan Kim and Renée Mauborgne, professors at INSEAD and co-directors of the INSEAD Blue Ocean Strategy Institute. The book argues that companies are better off swimming in less-crowded 'Blue Oceans' instead of the very crowded 'Red Oceans'.

The theory provides a four-action framework that consists of:

- **Raise:** This questions which factors must be raised within an industry in terms of product, pricing or service standards.
- **Eliminate:** This questions which areas of a company or industry could be completely eliminated to reduce costs and to create an entirely new market.

- **Reduce:** This questions which features or appendages of a company's product or service are not needed, but add to cost (for example, having a double-layered pack when one layer would do). Therefore, this can be reduced without completely eliminating it.
- **Create:** This prompts companies to be innovative with their products. By creating an entirely new product or service, a company can create its own market through differentiation from the competition.

Was it that the agency did not put across its point forcefully enough? Should we have gone back to the client with a better set of arguments? Should we have asked Mark to come back for yet another meeting? Would we have succeeded in our efforts? Again, I am not sure.

Interestingly when the Marketing Head of Lever Johnson, Gopalakrishnan, was leaving India (to take up a global position at S. C. Johnson USA), a couple of years after that momentous lunch and the meeting with Mark on LV, he admitted that when he had heard us say things like set up a small sales force, focus on liquid vaporisers, etc., he thought that we were speaking balderdash (as P. G. Wodehouse would put it). But thinking back he said that we were actually speaking in the best interests of the company. He regretted that he had not paid heed. In a small way, it was comforting to hear that from Gopalakrishnan, whom I believe is a very sound marketing strategist.

The lesson from this episode was that we should have built our arguments well and gone back for a second round and maybe, even a third round. There was no fear of the client sacking us then, the relationship between Chicago (FCB head office) and Racine (S. C. Johnson head office) was very firm at that time (unfortunately, FCB lost the SCJ account a decade later). While the relationship lasted, the FCB-SCJ association was indeed unique. Not only was the agency evaluated by the client, the client was evaluated by the agency. And all these reports found their way to Chicago and Racine ... and were taken seriously! If an SCJ client in a particular country was rated very badly by his FCB counterpart, he could be hauled up for not treating a valued partner fairly. Given the depth of the relationship, I wish we had done a better job. But, we did try.

Maybe we should have 'tried harder', as the famous campaign for Avis Rent-A-Car said.

The Chaiwala Test

How does one keep a client and not get caught in the intra-company cross fires that are *de rigueur* in the corporate world? This is a constant challenge for anyone who is in the client servicing profession. Be it advertising, marketing research, event management or even consulting, managing the multiple layers of a client organisation is not just a science, but also an art of great complexity.

Our agency had won the Zee account after a long pursuit. The company was going through some challenging times and the agency was hired with the explicit purpose of playing the role of a 'sounding board' and a 'strategic advisor', not just a creator of funny eye-catching ads. To some extent we had succeeded, but realised that *Dilli bahut door hai* (our destination was very far away).

As we began to understand organisational dynamics, we were told that Zee had a new CEO, and it was none other than the much-acclaimed, almost-revered media leader, Pradip Guha.

I had known Pradip Guha from my days as a lowly account executive in the late '70s and early '80s. I realised that Pradip's taste in advertising was very different from what our agency was known for. While he loved highly creative ads, our agency was focused on strategy-focused ads. We believed that while creative was extremely important, our playbook was that it was strategy that won the battle, not funny or creative ads. But I also knew that Pradip would be fair with what he did with the agency, as long as we delivered as per the brief and continued to add value.

But you can never be sure.

As can be expected we soon started to see a number of new faces in Zee. Some were very friendly with the agency, while some were openly antagonistic. The team handling the account—Nitin Karkare and Anita Gokral—had their plates full, managing the various turf and territory issues within the client organisation.

A media organisation is not a simple client to handle. You have to remember that they are in the business of media and are creating new content, day in and day out. These media organisations are also full of creative people, who write and evaluate scripts, shoot promotions and record spots for a living. Internally, they have their own areas of expertise and often all of them are in the same room to brief an agency and evaluate its work. These meetings could be a breeze or a nightmare.

Anita was extremely diligent and hardworking while Nitin brought his strategic insights into the account, given his strong understanding of the entertainment space. The account planning team worked long hours, churning out very useful analysis with the copious amounts of data that flows from the television measurement system. But we knew that we were tap dancing on quicksand.

I decided that I would make sure that I met Pradip one-on-one at least once a month. And before I would meet him, I would obtain a total debrief from the team. My logic was that if I was going to get shot at close quarters, I should know what shield I should use.

Before one such meeting, as Carol, Pradip's long-time assistant led me into his office, I knew that things were not going to be okay.

And sure as hell, Pradip started his feedback session in earnest after the initial exchange of pleasantries. He said, 'Ambi, you have to do something about the art you give us. The campaigns are working, but the art sucks.' And in his own inimitable style politely suggested, 'Do you want me to identify some good freelance art person to work on our account?'

I knew this question would come up and I probed to find out what he was so upset about and realised that he was speaking about the outdoor campaign that had been launched for one of their key shows. I had gone prepared. I politely asked him, 'Yes, I agree the outdoor ads look a little dated, but did you review what was presented to the team, before this was approved and put up?' He was not aware that the design that was up on the hoarding sites was in fact the twentieth iteration of what the agency had done. So I asked him, politely, if he would like to see the nineteen rejected iterations. He was not sure what was in store, but agreed to look at all the variations. I had carried A4 sized colour print outs of each of the nineteen variations.

As I began putting them on the table in front of him, I could see his eyes widen and he exclaimed, 'All this was presented to my team and they chose the one that went up on hoardings? Why?' I explained that the Zee team often over-corrected for the sophistication of the South Bombay types. The designs were dumbed down and made to look less 'classy' and more 'massy'. He was aghast that the team had not picked one of the more aesthetically designed ads. So in his characteristic style, he immediately called the head of marketing communication and asked her if she had seen all the variations. She confirmed that she had. He then asked her why she let the programme team choose the one design that went up on hoardings. She repeated the 'massy' vs 'classy' story. He asked her who are we to decide what is 'massy' and what is 'classy'.

Pradip had always had a sense of style and fashion (he had pioneered the Miss India contests and taken it to a new high). So he said let us ask the person who served tea (chaiwala) what he thought. The chaiwala walked in with my green tea and he was asked to choose the design he liked most. And as luck would have it, he picked the one which the Zee team had rejected in Round 2.

We thanked the chaiwala and got into a discussion on how we often tend to underestimate the aesthetic sense of the common man. We believe what will appeal to them will be crude designs, bright colours and bold lettering. But the 'massy' consumer is changing fast. They too are watching English television and Miss India shows. They too are visiting malls and walking past (if not shopping at) high-end designer stores. And their sense of taste is rapidly evolving. So Pradip explained to the Zee team that they had to be more sensitive to this before dumbing down what the agency presented.

I heaved a huge sigh of relief as I walked out of the Zee office that day. I also realised that may be there was a lesson for the agency too. How could we sell the creatives better, without getting the client all riled up about our rigid stance?

The agency's relationship with Zee lasted for a full ten years. We had our highs and lows. We produced some great advertising but most importantly, also played the role of a sounding board and strategic partner.

After Pradip Guha left Zee and Punit Goenka took over as the CEO, I did not stop my practice of meeting the CEO every month. Our meetings were sometimes in the office, but often at a watering hole. The meetings were highly informal and once Punit embarrassed me by saying, 'How come you have not criticised me on anything today?' It was such a strong relationship that we were allowed to criticise each other, at will. And I think that is what makes for a great partnership. The client on his side takes away the fear of failure from the agency and the agency is ready to take a stance and fight for what they truly believe to be important for the brand. We fought many battles together and a few with each other.

I can still remember Punit calling me on my mobile phone on the night of 26 November, 2008. I had been out of town and my flight had landed past 9 p.m. As soon as I got into my car, I got a call from Punit and he sounded worried, 'Sir, where are you? Hope you are okay?' I explained that I had just landed and my driver had mentioned something, but I was not sure what was happening.

Punit explained, 'There is a terror attack happening as we speak. Your office is just opposite the Trident. If there are people working in your office they should lock up the office and stay inside. Ask them not to get out till they watch the news and get an all clear sign.' I thanked him and added that there would be people working late in the office and may be some were working on his campaigns. The next call was to the office and the admin head. I need not have worried, the office was secure. The people in office had been alerted. The shutter was down and they were told to open up the pantry and eat what was available. I called Punit to confirm that all were safe.

That puts a different perspective on client-agency relationships, doesn't it? Punit was the CEO of the company. He need not have called me to find out if all were safe in the agency. He had a hundred other things to worry about. Yet, he did so as he realised that the agency tended to work late and could get caught in the crossfire. He was right, of course.

What makes for great client-agency relationships?

In the book *50 Rules to Keep a Client Happy*, Fred C. Poppe puts down some thumb rules. First is product knowledge; you should know as much about the client's product as he does. Keep the client informed, both about themselves and about the competition. Keep the client informed about what was happening in your company. Do the required reading. Be punctual always. Submit contact reports on time. Remember to wish the client on important days. Develop a client servicing personality and so thank everyone, irrespective of hierarchy (even the chaiwala as this story would have told you). Constant Contact. And more contact.

We tend to underestimate the importance of contact. Senior managers tend to believe that the front line is doing the job. But this is a fallacy. There has to be contact at every level of the organisation. The better-run service organisations develop a hierarchy of contacts so that there is regular contact across at least three levels of the organisation. Also, a contact cannot be just a drink or an environmental political chit-chat. Relationships are built only if at each level the contact is about business and concern for each other's wellbeing. We sometimes make the mistake of assuming that senior executives are not interested in knowing about the nitty-gritties of the business. We couldn't be more wrong. I have noticed that clients get impressed if the CEO of the service organisation knows what is happening and is ready to answer any questions that they may have. So it is critical to go to these 'catch-up meetings', fully prepared.

I had gone prepared to pass the Chaiwala Test. How prepared will you be when the chaiwala is called in to pass judgement on your plan? You have been warned.

Sorry. Please Leave!

Holidays in the India of the '70s and '80s meant a trip to the native home town or village, or to the favorite temple town. The elite of the country holidayed abroad. The only high-end destination the affluent, domestic traveller wanted to visit was Goa, Kashmir and Rajasthan.

In this scenario, in the year 1988 a small hotel group in Kochi, the Casino Group, bid for and won the contract to manage the only property constructed on a land that still remained untouched by the outside world—the Bangaram Island in Lakshadweep. This small group managed to outbid some of the biggest names in the industry, proving a number of naysayers wrong. In fact, Jose Dominic, CEO of CGH Earth (as the Casino Group of Hotels is known today) confessed to the reporter from *Outlook Business* (7 July 2017) that 'Had we failed to make a success out of the place, it would have jeopardised the existing property under the brand, and our ability to service the Rs 25 lakh loan sourced from Indian Bank.'

Not having the deep-pocket financial muscle of his competitors, Jose's idea was to make the project a low-budget one and to be completed rapidly. Defying the popular logic of that time, the Bangaram Island Resort under CGH would not be a plush property, but earthy and true-to-nature. In a big departure from the norms of the times, it would feature no telephones, no television sets, no multi-cuisine restaurants and air-conditioners. They would also avoid artificial flavours in their food, carbonated beverages or snacks in plastic packs.

The idea was to pitch the resort to the evolved traveller as 'nature in its most pristine form'. The list price for a room was $180 per night, equal to the prices charged by the super-deluxe hotels of Mumbai and Delhi, a jaw-dropping price in the late '80s.

The company realised that it would not be able to break even for anything less (there were only thirty cottages that could accommodate sixty adults). The tourists who opted for this exotic location had to spend a fortune to get to this remote place: fly down to Kochi from Mumbai or Delhi, and then take a flight to Agatti in Lakshadweep. From Agatti it was a one-and-a-half-hour boat ride to Bangaram Island.

The agency tasked to help Jose Dominic was FCB Ulka Advertising's Kochi branch (then called Ulka Advertising). The team in Kochi, Pradeep Bhaskaran and Joemon Thaliath were excited by the prospect of working with a tourism pioneer. Obviously, ad budgets were very limited. Quite rightly, the company wanted to do a lot of PR with the international tourism trade. But they did want to attract top-end Indian tourists too.

Finally, after much discussion they decided to spend all their budget in one colour ad in a leading business daily. The ad quite simply showed a scenic picture of the island with the rather intriguing headline 'Thank God, He Created Nothing'. The readers were told about this unique island and to know more they had to write to the Casino Group at Kochi. The company decided to not only send a colour brochure to all the respondents, but also a specially created film on Bangaram Island resort (in a VHS cassette—remember this was a pre-internet, pre-CD age).

The idea of doing an ad in the financial daily was as audacious as the venture itself. But what really blew me away was the commitment that CGH showed to the cause of creating possibly, India's first eco-friendly tourist resort.

On one of my visits to Cochin I got to speak with Jose Dominic about his passion for creating a unique tourist experience at Bangaram Island resort. He got talking about how he was empowering his entire organisation for this journey.

Apparently, a few weeks before I had met met , two very affluent families from North India had come to Bangaram, on a one-week holiday package. But as soon as they checked into the rooms, they discovered that the rooms were not air-conditioned. And there was no television. Also to their horror, they discovered they could not even get their favourite carbonated beverage. The kids in the family started creating a fuss and their parents joined them in their litany of woes, disturbing the other guests in the small resort.

The General Manager of the hotel had to take a call. Either he could mollycoddle the two families, and keep listening to their complaints right through their one-week stay. Or organise a television set (and soft drinks) from one of the other islands of Lakshadweep.

Or take the most drastic action that anyone from the hospitality industry hates to take: evict the guests.

Finally, the call was taken to request the guests to leave the premises by the next boat to Agatti. And the hotel, which was yet to break even, offered to pay for all the expenses that the guests had incurred, including the air travel cost, and also refund the full amount paid to the hotel.

Remember the hotel was a small property and it would have been impossible to get guests at the last minute to fill those empty rooms. But inspite of that, they were not willing to compromise on what they had set out to do.

When I heard this story, I think in 1990, I was convinced that this hotel group was destined to rewrite eco-friendly tourism in India. And that is exactly what happened. CGH now operates seventeen boutique hotels comprising 409 rooms across Kerala, Tamil Nadu and Karnataka.

Amitabh Kant, the current CEO of the government of India think-tank NITI Ayog and former tourism secretary of Kerala, credited with transforming the state into a premium holiday destination with the clarion call of 'Visit—God's Own Country!' has this to say about CGH Earth as the Casino Group is known today: 'CGH Earth is a great example of a local entrepreneur creating experiential hospitality that addresses the aspiration of the new age travellers.'

What I still recall about our association with Bangaram Resort/Casino Group was the commitment to ensure that they did not try and be what they were not. And they had the courage to stand up to a bully and take a loss in their stride.

Working in the service industry most of my life, I have had to face clients who had to be told where to get off (this book too has a story or two). I learnt a very valuable lesson from Jose Dominic and the CGH Earth Group. If you are committed to your vision, you cannot allow anyone, even a premium paying customer, to derail you.

Simon Sinek is a British-American author and motivational speaker. His talk *Start With Why—How Great Leaders Inspire Action* is listed as one of the top three TED talks of all time. He created the concept of the 'Golden Circle'. The core of the circle is 'Why'. The next layer is 'How' and the outermost layer is 'What'. He explains how organisations are often obsessed with what they make: products, services, things. They spend little time in putting down 'why' they do what they do. He says that the highly successful companies often start with a 'why': what is the purpose of the organisation, what are its beliefs, what is the cause it is chasing. They then figure out the 'how': the processes that need to be followed. And finally they work on the 'what': what are the products and services they can offer. At the end of his short TED talk he convinces us that people don't buy what you do, they buy why you do it. Great leaders inspire people to do things that inspire them.

Purpose-driven leadership is what set apart a terrific leader like Jose Dominic.

In his book *Discover Your True North*, Bill George points out that, 'Just as a compass points towards a magnetic field, your True North pulls you towards the purpose of your leadership. When you follow your internal compass, your leadership will be authentic, and people will naturally want to associate with you'. The book captures the lessons learnt from 125 top CEOs and Bill George, who himself was a much-acclaimed CEO of Medtronic. The book presents a five step self-development plan:

- Knowing your authentic self
- Defining your values and leadership principles
- Understanding your motivations
- Building your support team
- Staying grounded by integrating all aspects of your life.

Would I have had the courage to evict the noisy tourists from my newly-built eco-friendly tourist resort? Or would I have tried to find a via media solution? Even as I write this, I am surprised that the small hotel took that bold call. Not many in their place would have been willing to forego the revenue.

There was also another lesson in that story. Obviously, they did not 'screen' the guests before they accepted the booking. Would they have avoided this embarrassment if they had explained all these facts to the guests as they were booking their room (remember it is too late to explain it after they check into the hotel—the nearest hotel is after all, a long boat ride away)?

In any business we are faced with clients who make extraordinary demands and make a huge amount of noise as well. But think, if you are able to set right their expectations early in the game, you may not end up in a messy situation.

Finally, you have to be ready to say, 'No, that is enough.' Not saying it will cause more damage than saying it at the appropriate time. A valuable lesson learnt.

Red & White ...
and Brown!

It had been a tough day. As the youngest and the junior-most member of the team I was stuck with all the 'tough' jobs of the agency. Chasing the production manager so that the material for the print ad got out on time. Pleading with the art director and then the studio manager and studio artists to finish the work so that it could go for pre-press production work. Getting newspapers to agree to allot space on their most important page. That was the nature of my beat.

It was the year 1981 and as must be clear, the Account Executive (AE) in an agency played many roles. But the ones detailed above weren't the only roles I played. Those were the days before media had been spun off into an independent business operation. Account planning or strategic planning was something that an AE did as routine. The agency I was working in also insisted that the AE should also do the media planning and even film negotiations with producers. It was a tough job but immensely satisfying. In the three years I spent as a lowly AE, I must have learnt more than what I learnt in the next six years. The sheer variety of clients and the myriad problems one faced were all a learning. Also the ad agency world was very different in the early '80s and the job of an AE was truly multi-dimensional.

But this is not a story about my grand escapades or successes. This is the story of Red & White ... and Brown!

Our agency had been tasked with launching the Red & White Filter Kings cigarettes in Mumbai. The brand was a big seller in Rajasthan, Haryana, eastern Uttar Pradesh (UP) and Delhi. The company, Godfrey Philips of India (GPI), had a strong presence in Mumbai through its Four Square Filter Kings (India's first king-size filter cigarettes). They wanted to strengthen their position in Mumbai by launching Red & White Kings at a lower price point. The idea was that if this extension did well, the company would be able to launch regular filter cigarettes as a follow-up measure.

The CEO of the company, Mr Kirit Vaidya was a seasoned veteran in the consumer packaged space, having spent many years at Horlicks/Beecham. He was also an alumnus of IIM Ahmedabad—the first batch in fact. His batch mates included Diwan Arun Nanda, the founder of the agency I was working in (Rediffusion Advertising) as well as other luminaries like the management guru, C. K. Prahlad (an interesting aside: it was Diwan Arun Nanda who won the Gold Medal at IIM the year he graduated, not C. K. Prahlad).

Mr Vaidya, though he was the CEO of the company was closely involved with the launch preparations. The Marketing Manager Shanawaz Bakht, also an IIMA alumnus, was a tobacco industry veteran, but Mr Vaidya wanted to shake up the system and put the company on a new trajectory.

The Mumbai launch of Red & White was a critical one for the company. It was the biggest king-size filter cigarette market. In those days, cigarette advertising was permitted in print, cinema and in outdoor media (only Doordarshan did not accept tobacco advertising; though pan masalas were kosher).

Then as now, ITC was the giant in the cigarette market everywhere and Mumbai was no exception. If you thought it was the party that that GPI feared, no, there was someone else as well.

Those were the days when the retailers of cigarette had huge clout in the marketplace. Companies had to seek their approval before launching a new brand. Today, the same is true with modern trade (companies have to synchronise their new launches with the calendars of large modern trade players; smaller players have to pay a 'carriage fee' to get them to stock their products). Back in the '80s, not only were the paan-beediwalas unionised, but their union was very powerful, and could even kill a launch before it was executed.

GPI knew about the complexities of the market and they had many seasoned veterans in the company whom Mr Vaidya consulted before the launch. The final plans were all ready. Cigarettes were being rolled out from the Chakala, Andheri factory. Space was booked in *Times of India* and other leading papers. Outdoor advertising sites had all been lined up. Posters were printed and ready. The print ads were ready to roll.

That fateful day, the agency team had been to the client office in the morning for a final sign-off. There had been a big debate on the display of the price of the cigarette in the advertising. The agency team was worried that the display of the price would antagonise the pan beedi trade. But, Mr Vaidya was adamant. He argued that the brand was aiming to create a new price point in the king-size cigarette market, and if the price was not displayed, a tepid message would go through.

Paan-beedi merchants in Mumbai were not too supportive of the MRP (Maximum Retail Price) mention of brands. Since they sold most of the cigarettes as loose sticks, they set their own price, often marking up by 10 to 20 per cent against the set MRP. Their argument was that they ended up losing one stick per pack due to the tobacco falling off. Since tobacco companies did not compensate them for the loss of sticks, they felt they should be allowed to set the price.

We knew of these dynamics and tried arguing with Mr Vaidya about the danger of displaying the MRP in the large print ads. Since he would not listen, we relented and agreed to include the price in the ad that was slated to appear the next morning.

I had rushed back to office to ensure the artworks were corrected, the price mentioned, production material made and rushed to Times of India before their 5 p.m. deadline.

It was 4 p.m. when I was interrupted by a call. Mr Vaidya was on the line. He asked for me, not for my boss or his super boss, who was an IIM buddy of Mr Vaidya. I almost stood up when I heard his voice. He said, 'Please remove the price from the ad.' I tried telling him that we were way past the deadline and so it would be impossible, unless we pushed the date of the ad by a day. But I promised to try my best to ensure that it happened. What he said next surprised me. He said he would meet me in our office to see if he could be of help.

I tried telling him that his coming to the small office of the agency (it was a very small office in Readymoney Terrace in Worli, Mumbai) was perhaps not necessary and that he need not bother himself with this forty-minute ride from Andheri to Worli. But he said he would come anyway.

The next thirty minutes were a flurry of phone calls and running up and down the stairs to the various departments. Artwork change. Artwork to block positive makers. Pleading with *Times of India* for an extension of deadline and so on. Soon, Mr Vaidya was in the office. He peeped into my little cubicle to ask, 'Do you need any help?'

As the dust settled, we managed to get all the ducks in a row and the ad appeared the next day, without the price. The brand launch was a success and the paan-beedi sellers accepted the brand with open arms.

Some weeks later as I thought back, I realised how touched I was by Mr Vaidya's gesture. He was the CEO of the company. It was his prerogative to decide what to put in an ad and what to take out. He had a team working with him and his team was a competent one. But why did he have to make the trip to meet the agency executive, who was a few million miles below him in the organisational hierarchy?

I think Mr Vaidya wanted to make a statement that he was pleading guilty for causing so much misery in my life. He wanted to let me know that he understood the thankless job I was doing and how he was willing to lend a helping hand.

Martin Seligman pioneered the concept of Positive Psychology and in his book *Authentic Happiness*, he presents the concept of twenty-four strengths. You too can take a test free of cost at the site* and figure out your top six strengths.

The twenty-four strengths are grouped into six sets: Wisdom and Knowledge, Courage, Humanity, Justice, Temperance and Transcendence. The Humanity vertical consists of Love, Kindness and Social Intelligence. Justice consists of Teamwork, Fairness and Leadership. And Temperance consists of Forgiveness, Humility, Prudence and Self-regulation. Wisdom and Knowledge consists of Creativity, Curiosity, Grit, Love of Learning and Perspective. Courage consists of Bravery, Perseverance, Honesty and Zest. Transcendence consists of Appreciation of Beauty, Gratitude, Hope, Humour and Spirituality.

I think Mr Vaidya displayed an amazing level of humility, social intelligence and fairness.

---

* https://ppc.sas.upenn.edu/resources/questionnaires-researchers/survey-character-strengths

That is what sets great leaders apart, their ability to accept their mistakes as their own, and move forward through a show of humility and social intelligence.

Think back. How often have you accepted a mistake as your own and made amends? The human tendency is to try and fob off the blame on someone else. But it takes a great deal of humility to stand up and accept the mistake and offer to make amends.

While the 'Red & White' part of the title is probably clear, you are probably wondering why Brown. Brown is the colour associated with earth, sand and mud. It is also the colour associated with humility. So I thought it would be a good addition to the brand name whose story has been narrated in this chapter.

India's First CEO CM

My colleague from Hyderabad, Dhruv Jha, was on the line wanting an urgent word. He excitedly explained that the agency team had been invited to present its thoughts on the launch of the new proposed technology township, HITEC City (Hyderabad Information Technology and Engineering Consultancy City) to the Chief Minister (CM) of Andhra Pradesh, Mr Chandrababu Naidu and his Chief Secretary the following week, and he wanted me to be there at the presentation.

The Hyderabad offices of ad agencies don't get too many big opportunities or clients to pitch for. The bigger clients are happy to work with Mumbai-based agencies. The smaller ones are difficult to manage, especially in terms of collections. Or at least that was the track record of our agency. Working with the government calls for a totally new set of skills and as an agency, we were not particularly good at this.

I requested Dhruv to rope in the Bangalore office team to work on the strategy and creative. We had a rare copywriter in Bangalore who was extremely digital-savvy and I felt he could be a good person to handle this pitch. But as for my going to Hyderabad … well, I was not sure.

Presenting to government bodies comes with its own

challenges. The dates tend to get changed at short notice. The forum that will sit in on the presentation is very fluid. One may make a trip from another city only to present to a lower-level secretary as the seniors have been pulled into other meetings. Further, meetings rarely start on time and often more than ten agencies are called to present, each being rationed out ten minutes to present their credentials, strategy for the campaign and creative layouts and scripts. These shoot-outs, or swayamvars, as we called them produce strange bedfellows. A smaller agency that had political connections could suddenly be seen pitching against the big boys. This formal pitch is likely just for show and the 'real pitch' is likely to be happening in a cabin next door.

I made up my mind that I would not travel to Hyderabad and waste my time. It was enough that the team in Hyderabad and some folks in Bangalore were sweating over it. I felt, probably wrongly, that my presence would not make an iota of difference to the outcome.

Two days before the date of the presentation I got an urgent call from our Hyderabad Media Manager, Sathyanarayana. Sathie, as he was fondly called was very upset with me. He told me in no uncertain terms that it was critical that I should show up for the big pitch. Remember, it was 1998 and I was ill-informed about his CM, Mr Naidu. I refused to budge. I asked him how sure he was that we would get to meet the CM. Would the CM sit through the presentation? Would he appreciate the ideas we presented? Would the selection of the agency be based on merit and only merit? The questions I had were numerous, but Sathie maintained his litany that I *had* to come to Hyderabad. I don't remember what finally made me change my mind, but I decided to make the trip. I also resolved that I would not waste company resources by spending an extra day in that city. I would travel back to Mumbai the same day, after the presentation.

On the day of the presentation, all of us met in the Hyderabad office and reviewed the presentation that had been crafted by Raj Alexander of Bangalore. I had wanted them to include a wonderful film produced for the city of Chicago by Foote Cone Belding (FCB), Chicago; it featured some great singing and wonderful visuals of the city. Somehow, I thought the presentation of a campaign for a global city would resonate with the CM.

As was to be expected we got a message from the CM's office that the CM was running late and we needed to be at the presentation venue at 3.30 p.m. and not 2.30 p.m. as originally scheduled. 'I told you so', I announced.

In our enthusiasm we got to the venue at 3 p.m. and were told that another agency was presenting and would be through in twenty minutes. We were ushered into the large conference room at 3.25 p.m. To my dismay, I saw the CM already seated.

Agencies do not want the client to be in the room when they are setting up. Often the setting up process, checking if the laptop and multimedia projector were compatible could take fifteen minutes (this problem continues to dog me as I struggle with the compatibility issues between the multimedia projector and my Apple MacBook). Then there is the audio system, which also needs to be connected and tested.

I did the smart thing, or so I thought, and sat next to the CM. He politely enquired where I was from. I explained that I was originally from Chennai but was now based at the head office in Mumbai and that our agency was a part of the global FCB agency network. The CM thanked me for coming all the way for the presentation and I in turn thanked him for giving us the opportunity to present. He then asked how long the presentation would take. I told him our team had done a lot of work, and would need forty minutes. He asked if we could finish the presentation in thirty minutes.

In the late '90s, getting a laptop connected to a projector used to be a complicated affair. But in the office of the CM of Andhra Pradesh it happened in two minutes. My team signalled that they were ready to go even as I finished my short introduction to Mr Naidu.

The presentation began. Privately, I wondered when the CM or one of his Secretaries would get up to 'take an urgent call'. To my surprise the CM and his entire team of senior Secretaries stayed glued to the presentation for the next thirty-odd minutes.

We had outlined a rather risky strategy of doing a live webcast of the launch of HITEC City by then Prime Minister Mr Atal Bihari Vajpayee. No one had attempted a live webcast of any event in India, till that date. The CM got the basic idea behind what was recommended. He realised that launching HITEC City had to be visible to the global diaspora of Andhraites.

The pitch ended well or so we thought. But we were not sure what the final outcome would be. As in all government contracts, we were aware that many other forces would be at play.

A few days later, our Hyderabad office got the confirmation that we had the assignment and Sathie was convinced that my presence had made a difference (till date I am not sure if it made an iota of a difference). I think I had underestimated the professionalism of Mr Naidu. I am convinced that he would have selected the agency even if I had not been there at the presentation.

The campaign consisted of print advertising, outdoor advertising and the live webcast. The webcast was a challenge since we had to take the help of a specialist digital vendor based out of Chandigarh. The internet pipe had to be provided through a leased line by VSNL.

Finally, all the moving parts came together. I could see the inauguration of HITEC City from my home in Mumbai (no, I did not make the trip to Hyderabad for the event!).

Many believe that the launch of HITEC City was a tipping point in the rise of Hyderabad and its being branded 'Cyberabad'. Legend has it that Phase I of HITEC City was completed in a record fourteen months. It was all done by a CM who behaved like a CEO.

It was later that I got to hear of yet another story about Mr Naidu and how he managed to get the Indian School of Business to Hyderabad. Apparently, the founding fathers of ISB wanted it to be based in the commercial capital of the country. But some unreasonable demands were made of them. Dejected, they reached out to Andhra Pradesh, not sure what kind of welcome they would receive. They were requested to come to Hyderabad as soon as they could.

What happened in Hyderabad is something that should go into the record books. As their cars drove into the Secretariat, they were received by the CM at the lobby. A huge signal to the team that they were more than welcome. They got all that they asked for and more. ISB was set up from foundation stone to inauguration in a record twenty-four months, a feat acknowledged and lauded by the then-PM Vajpayee when he inaugurated the campus.

Corporate India tends to view politicians and bureaucrats with jaundiced eyes. But CM Naidu was a trendsetter in many ways. He behaved not like a CM but as a CEO who was set on changing the dynamics of the state. The fact that today there are more Telugu-speaking engineers in Silicon Valley and they outnumber Tamils who were number one earlier, is all because of his visionary leadership and drive to put Andhra on the global IT Map.

Today, if you visit Hyderabad's HITEC City Phase I, it looks like a quaint little building. It is out-ranked by numerous other towers—housing international IT majors like Microsoft, IBM, Cisco and Oracle as also Indian giants like TCS, Wipro, Infosys, Tech Mahindra and HCL. In 1998, the lone building in that IT

Corridor was the HITEC City building. It is amazing to see the transformation that can happen when a CM behaves like a CEO who is trying to maximise the opportunities that his people have, to become more successful, more wealthy and more happy.

As a service provider, I learnt a valuable lesson. I should not have jumped to conclusions without knowing more about the person in the client's chair. On all counts I turned out to be wrong. The meeting started almost on time. We got sufficient time to present our recommendations. The CM sat through the meeting without any disturbance (in fact, in the 2000s no meeting takes place where the chief decision maker pays undivided attention to the presentation, what with the mobile phone being a constant distraction). The questions asked at the end were pertinent and to the point. The final decision was taken in our favour despite the fact that we were a political nobody in the state. The support for the final live webcast was all there, and there was no finger pointing when it was happening. Finally, our bills got paid on time.

I wonder how much can be achieved if all our CMs behave like CEOs. Don't get me wrong. I don't want them to be quarter-on-quarter profit maximisers. But if they can work towards a vision for the transformation of their state, take decisions based on merit, not on connections, and stay the course once the decisions are made, we will be a different country.

As they say, it is easier said than done. In politics, there are multiple forces pulling you in different directions. But with the country having completed seventy years of existence as an independent nation, I see light at the end of the tunnel. More and more CMs are behaving like CEOs, going beyond their narrow political remit and looking at the larger picture. Hopefully, we will see a different India when the country hits the seventy-five year mark. As the late genius John Lennon said, 'You may say I'm a dreamer, but I am not the only one.'

Reading Smoke Signals

Launching a new product brings with it a whole lot of challenges. When we were asked to launch India's first private sector mutual fund, we had to do some quick learning. In the mutual funds sector, Unit Trust of India, the public sector behemoth was the pioneer. But the opportunities were vast and the client we had bagged had excellent credentials. Not only were they a well-connected Indian group, they also had an excellent American mutual fund or asset management corporation (AMC) as their partner. I don't know how we got the account, but I suppose the client, Vivek Reddy, had heard something nice about us from some common friends.

The launch was back-breaking and the small team in Chennai worked day and night for six weeks to ensure all that was needed was done. The team from Mumbai flew down to present the campaigns. The team in Chennai executed the work well, or so I thought.

The launch of the fund happened well and the issue was fully subscribed as expected.

But we were in for a shock soon after. Vivek called me and told me that he was moving his business to a different agency. I asked him if it was because he now had a new Chief Marketing Officer (CMO) who had an agency background. Vivek said that was not the only reason. He thought we had executed everything well, maybe a little too well. He did not expect the level of service he got from us. But, he thought we were a little too willing to please. He felt that we delivered everything so much on time that he was left wondering if we were not doing the best we could. Were we compromising on quality in our pursuit of timely delivery?

There was no option for me to wriggle out. The die had been cast. So I patiently listened to what he had to say and left.

In yet another incident, the agency was sacked by a large telecom firm. This was an account for whom the agency had done trail-blazing work and won Grand Effies.[*] The CEO was a friend and I had met him when he had taken over the company from his predecessor (who had hired the agency). So I decided to call him to understand why. What he told me was surprising. He was honest enough to admit that the agency had built the brand, but had we not seen the smoke signals coming out of the client organisation for the previous twelve months? He told me that he thought we would put in place mechanisms to handle the discontent with the agency. And he also, (this was unsaid, but I think this is what he meant), expected someone from the agency to reach out to him to take his views. We had failed to do that.

Fortunately for me, I have not had the dishonour of being sacked too often. In fact, FCB Ulka had a reputation for picking up accounts and growing with them for decades. The industry knew this and that kept them away from poaching our accounts.

But we did lose accounts.

---

[*] The Grand Effies are given by Effie Worldwide and stand for effectiveness in marketing communications, spotlighting marketing ideas that work and encouraging thoughtful dialogue about the drivers of marketing effectiveness.

The question arises, therefore: how do agencies lose accounts even after doing stellar work on large brands for years?

In the article 'Developing an Account Management Lifecycle for Advertising Agency—Client Relationship', David Waller (in the magazine *Marketing Intelligence and Planning*) has created a theory of a lifecycle. This consists of three stages: AGENCY EVALUATION AND SELECTION; RELATIONSHIP DEVELOPMENT AND MAINTENANCE; AND AGENCY REVIEW AND TERMINATION. He points out that the main reasons for termination are success/failure issue, creative issue, cost issue, and interpersonal issue.

I found the explanation of 'how relationships break down' to be very insightful. It all starts with a sense of 'creeping disenchantment'. This leads to weak and then strong 'signals of dissatisfaction', finally leading to a 'breakdown in communication'. David Waller has quite rightly observed that, 'The criteria for selecting an agency is different from the criteria used to decide whether to keep the agency; for example, the role of creative diminishes as the client-agency relationship evolves.'

In the service industry, there are several tenets that have stood the test of time.

The first is that it is rare to win a pitch if you are hearing about the pitch itself from an email you get from the prospective client. The better players, be it in advertising or in IT services, are there in the client's offices even before the Request for Proposal (RFP) has been put together. The earlier you are in the arena, the better the chance of winning the pitch. Of course, in many government contracts, the influential vendor can put conditions in the RFP that only a few can fulfill. This ensures that the vendor wins the contract almost by default.

Winning the pitch calls for a different set of skills. At least in advertising, in addition to the work being presented, there is a need for drama and excitement, for theatre and play acting. Clients like it. As one client told me after we were given the not-so-good news: 'You guys were good, but those guys were willing to spill blood for us.' As if anyone would!

Managing a client calls for a different set of skills. You have to be in a position to hear the signals of 'creeping disenchantment'. How do you manage that? The team on the ground, which meets the client every other day, are often not in a position to pick up these signals. This has to be understood and managed better. It is important that the client is engaged with at multiple levels. If the frontline servicing team meets the client brand team every week, the GM on the account should meet the head of marketing, one-on-one, at least once a month. And the CEO of the agency has to meet the CEO of the client organisation once a quarter.

These multiple levels of contact help build multiple bridges from the client to the agency. In addition, if the client works with several divisions of the agency, you get more signals to read and interpret.

Going back to the mutual fund story, I think the mistake made by the agency was that they had a single point contact at the highest level, but they ignored the changing landscape below that level. This must have antagonised the client organisation, and altered its perception of the agency, leading to the firing.

The other case was simply one of not engaging with the client at multiple levels. The agency was overconfident of the work that it had done on the brand. It thought it was invincible. In fact, even the industry thought so; and several agencies refused to pitch for the account thinking that the account was unshakeable. Because of this over-confidence, the agency team did not engage with multiple levels of the client organisation. There were signals coming out, but they were not being read and were being dismissed as false signals. If we had engaged with the client at multiple levels, we may have understood the 'signals of dissatisfaction' and the 'breakdown of communication', and may have salvaged the account. This was the playbook that had powered the growth of the agency for well over two decades, but somewhere the playbook was forgotten, leading to the loss of the account.

Can I blame the client for not having made a stronger complaint? Why did they not raise the dissatisfaction issue to a higher level? But then again, why should they?

Often, ad agencies and I should say, all service providers are caught in a dilemma. The ground-level operational team is not too happy if the higher echelons of the agency has an independent dialogue with the higher layers of the client organisations. There is a sense of insecurity. 'My marketing manager will get upset if you go and meet the CEO, without his presence…' is a common lament. But the CEO will not open up if the marketing manager is in the same room.

How is this barrier to be overcome? One habit I had developed was a one-on-one lunch (or drinks) meeting, on a regular basis with some key clients. To make this even more interesting we never went to the same restaurant twice. This was sometimes even referred to as the 'special gourmet lunch' or 'oenophile evening'. But the clients whom I managed to go to these gourmet lunches with did stay happy with the agency. We also managed to pick up signals of discontent even before the smoke signals came out, all over some tasty dimsums!

Architects and Pillars

It was a hot summer day and the Ulka office at Nirmal Building in Nariman Point wore a deserted look. The receptionist was woken from her slumber by an elderly-looking gentleman in a safari suit. He wanted to meet the Chairman of the company, Mr Bal Mundkur. Since Bal was not in the office, he asked for the next-in-command. That person, the Joint Managing Director, was not in office either. The receptionist, now fully awake, soon realised that this was an important person. She quickly found who she thought was the smartest of the young lot in office, Shashi Sinha, and called him urgently to the conference room even as she made sure that the guest was made comfortable.

That was how Shashi Sinha met Dr Varghese Kurian, the 'Milk Man of India', the Chairman of the National Dairy Development Board (NDDB) and Gujarat Co-operative Milk Marketing Federation (GCMMF) and the man behind the 'Amul' brand. (Shashi continues till date to be a great fan of Dr Kurien.)

As it transpired, Dr Kurian was in the Nirmal building for another meeting. While waiting for the elevator, he noticed that the building housed an Indian ad agency, Ulka Advertising. He enquired with his colleague, if Ulka was a reputed agency. And he got an answer in the affirmative. So he thought he should visit the agency on his way down and see if Amul could work with them.

Shashi realised the importance of the visitor, apologised profusely for the absence of the Chairman, MD, et al. Dr Kurian was extremely understanding and suggested that the Ulka team visit Anand the next week for a formal meeting. 'Maybe you could end up getting Amul as a client', was his throwaway line. As if we needed one!

As they say, the rest is history. Ulka ended up starting work with Amul on the Amulya Dairy whitener brand. The relationship grew and the agency managed to handle a large part of the expanding portfolio of Amul. Dr Kurian is no more but the team that continues to run GCMMF are living by the credo that was laid down by Dr Kurian.

Right from the days of Dr Kurian, it was an annual custom for the agency to present its next year's campaign plans to the Chairman and the team. The agency team works for months to put together the ad campaigns and no stone is left unturned in search of a better idea.

The story goes that in one of those meetings, the agency presented its campaign ideas. As always Dr Kurian asked, what the agency's recommendation was. The agency team pointed to, let us call it, Campaign A. At that stage, one of the team members of Amul piped up to say that he too liked the campaign, but felt that the colour or the font was not appropriate. He wanted the agency to make some major changes to the campaign.

It was then that Dr Kurian gave his 'architect and pillars' story. He told the young man, if you are building a house and the architect has given you the design, you like it, but you feel there are too many pillars and you ask the architect to remove some of the pillars. A few years later, your house falls on your head, whom do you blame? The architect or yourself?

So instead of asking for a change in colour or font, he asked the youngster to articulate his concerns: was the font not readable enough; was the colour not a 'food' colour, etc. The agency should then be asked to provide its answers. If the answers were not satisfactory, the solution may be to go back to the drawing board, instead of removing a few pillars.

It is no wonder that Amul built great relationships with its agency partners. The Amul butter hoardings are created by DaCunha Advertising, an agency that has had these duties for many decades. The agency team creates these topical ads and these go up on hoardings, even before they are approved by the client team. The trust between the agency and client is so strong and the respect for each others' domain expertise is so complete that the agency is treated as a co-owner of the brand. I don't think there is any other large brand, in any other country, where the client sees the ad message along with the target consumers.

The Amul topicals are a great example for brands who are struggling to stay current in social media. At a conference, I asked a digital marketing manager of a healthcare company how many days it took for his company to approve a social media post and he sheepishly said, 'Twenty-three days!' Imagine, the message goes through five layers in India and then goes to the UK office, again five layers, before it comes back with an 'OK' stamp. By the time the message is approved, it is probably no longer topical.

Dr Kurien also had a great sense of humour and a way to address problems. As the head of NDDB, he was also tasked with leading the oil revolution. One of the things he did was to launch an oil brand 'Dhara'. The agency handling this business was Mudra, Ahmedabad. They then made one of my all-time favourite ads for the brand.

In this ad a little kid is sitting alone in a small town railway station, looking a little forlorn. He suddenly spots 'Ramu Kaka', the friendly old postman. He shouts out 'Ramu Kaka', to which the old postman, who is playacting all along asks, 'Arre Bablu, you are here? Why?'

The little kid replies, 'Everyone shouts at me. So I am running away from home.' Ramu Kaka then entices him by saying, 'But why are you running away today? Your mom is making hot hot jalebis at home.'

The kid exclaims, 'Jalebis!' The next scene we see is of him being taken home on Ramu Kaka's old bicycle. There is a hot plate of jalebis waiting for young Bablu. Ramu Kaka then takes leave. The mom asks Bablu, 'So when are you running away next?' to which the smiling father replies, 'Maybe twenty years later!'

The ad is a masterpiece, with so much embedded in it and the brand is at the core of the story. It seems soon after the ad broke on television, there was a news report in a paper in Punjab that a kid was spotted in a small-town railway station running away from home, because his mom was not making jalebis! The team at NDDB and the agency wanted to flag this to Dr Kurien. They were wondering what he would say. They need not have worried. Dr Kurien's comment was, 'So the ad is working. Keep running it!'

Dr Kurien was able to trust his partners and nurture great relationships, in all the organisations he oversaw.

Trust is a two-way street. You cannot blindly trust anyone. But if you feel the other party is worthy of your trust, you should make the first move to offer trust. You may be surprised at the response.

The *Thirukural* is a classic ancient Tamil text of verse on virtues, wealth, love life and human relations. The *Kural* as it is popularly known consists of 1330 couplets or 'kurals', dealing with the everyday virtues of an individual. Considered one of the greatest works ever written on ethics and morality, chiefly secular ethics, it is known for its universality and non-denominational nature. It was authored by Valluvar, also known as Thiruvalluvar.

The text has been dated variously from 300 BCE to the 7th century CE. There are more than fifty couplets that outline how to manage trust, how to evaluate and then trust. Let me share one:

This task he can do, using these resources—
once you reason it out thus, leave the task to him.

All of us can be found guilty of asking an architect to drop a few pillars. Dr Kurian's little parable is a great reminder for us to remember the perils of meddling with what should be an expert's domain. But as the *Thirukural* points out, we need to ascertain that 'this task he can do, using these resources'. Once you do that, you should leave the job to the experts, instead of meddling in their task.

This is a lot easier said than done, especially in the Indian context. We have a work culture that disrespects time. A car that goes into a repair shop never comes out the day it was promised. The plumber never appears when he is supposed to appear. And you may well ask, who are you asking me to 'trust'?

Trust is a two-way street as we saw. And it starts in small doses. Can we demonstrate greater trust and see if that can change behaviour?

I got a taste of this recently. My photo lab, where I get photo albums made (yes, the old-fashioned ones), was supposed to have an album ready. But in the past, I had made it a point to visit them twice to check the layout. So this time round they were waiting for my second visit and hadn't finished the task. So who should I blame for the delay? Me or the lab?

Look back and see if there are other such examples from your own life. Can you demonstrate a greater degree of trust? And what will that entail? What will you lose?

And more importantly, what will you gain?

Better-designed houses, with the right number of pillars, probably.

Biases, Biases, Biases

Working with a public-sector unit calls for a different mindset. Some service organisations manage the environment much better than others. I for one was not a big fan. Till the following incident happened.

An ad agency is only as good as the new business it wins. If an agency is not able to win new business, rest assured, it will start losing business. This is probably true in all service industries, but more pronounced in sectors where the entry moat is wide. So once you get a client, he will not be able to leave that easily (this was true in India at least till the early 2000s).

New business is like a lifeline. It helps drive new energy into the organisation. People are willing to burn the midnight oil for a new business pitch. Most ad agencies, like other service organisations have ways and means of pitching for new business. One obvious way is to identify new entrants into the market and try to meet them, by cold calling. Another is to create an event, like a seminar or a party and invite prospects to the event.

The case of public sector companies is a little different. Most of them go through a periodic overhaul of their agency relationships.

So if your agency is among the top ten or top twenty, chances are you will get invited to a pitch, if you have been in touch. Often the people you have to be in touch with are a few rungs below the key decision-makers, unlike in private sector companies. So the new business chase in a PSU calls for a very different orientation. For one, keeping in touch with real (and not feigned) enthusiasm is a must. Feigned enthusiasm is visible and not appreciated. Then comes the opportunity to pitch. PSU pitches often involve five or even ten agencies. So it ends up being a toss-up as to who will win the pitch. The people who you had diligently followed up with may or may not have a casting vote. And sometimes the person at the top may have a bias.

Given all this, I was not a fan. But the team at the agency I was running, FCB Ulka, managed to keep track of key PSUs and even got us invited for a few big PSU pitches. Tracking PSU pitches is a job by itself and involves keeping an eye on the news. As the following story will tell you.

My colleague Kinjal Medh and I were discussing new business and he mentioned that something was happening at Unit Trust of India. This was the largest mutual fund player (at that time) that had helped middle-income Indians benefit from the stock market boom through some innovative schemes. The company continued to do well later in spite of the market being opened up to private sector players. I was involved with the launch of India's first private sector mutual fund (Kothari Pioneer) in 1993, so I knew a little bit about the business.

Unit Trust of India was then embroiled in a big scam. It was in the public eye and the government was forced to take action against its MD and also air-drop a seasoned bureaucrat to manage the mess. Newspapers were full of news about the imminent demise of Unit Trust of India.

Kinjal mentioned that he had been in touch with Unit Trust of

India and the team there was very receptive to his views on what they needed to do. My anti-PSU bias kicked in and I pooh-poohed the idea of chasing the Unit Trust account. I told him it would be a total waste of time and we ought to go after potential private sector companies. Kinjal said nothing.

A day later though, he casually mentioned that we needed to go to Unit Trust to meet the new Chairman and Managing Director (CMD). I was surprised. I had read that Mr M. Damodaran was being appointed as the CMD, but would he really have the time to meet the agency? Here was an IAS officer who had served in the north-eastern states and later in the Central Government finance ministry. Would he really meet us?

Hunger for new business got the better of me. We started working on what we needed to present to Mr Damodaran. A kind of a relaunch strategy for Unit Trust of India.

We went to the meeting with a fair degree of trepidation. I have been in several such situations in PSU meetings and often, the CMD failed to appear. On a few occasions, he gave a cursory five-minute darshan before rushing off to take a call from 'Delhi'.

This meeting however, was different.

We set up our short presentation and Mr Damodaran was with us in a few minutes. We had done our homework, knew that he loved to read and was a football fanatic. Kinjal's comments about soccer got him in a good mood. He listened to us and then informed us that he was going to change the brand to UTI Mutual Fund and had a logo ready for us to work with. He then asked us, 'How quickly can you come with an ad?' We mentioned we would need a week, for us to do a little more investor research and then do the creatives. Based on that, the next meeting date was fixed.

As I left the meeting, Kinjal and I bet on whether the next meeting would or would not happen the following week. In fact, in all likelihood, I reckoned, it would not happen at all.

But I was wrong. The UTI team called us the next day to confirm the date and time for the next meeting.

We trooped in a week later with a four-ad campaign. We had done our analysis of UTI and its strengths. Its technology. Its team of agents. And its huge family of investors. We realised that if UTI's investors were to be fitted into 'a country', that country could be one of the biggest in the world. From here was born the campaign idea 'Welcome to UTI Country'. We knew we had a good campaign, but again my PSU bias was kicking in hard. Would they really buy this campaign? That too in full-page, glorious colour, to be run in all the national newspapers?

The meeting with the CMD went wonderfully well. He loved our idea and the campaign. He said he wanted to send a message into the market that it was the beginning of a new UTI that would live up to its promises. The restructuring exercise was in progress and he was sure the timing was right. He had one critical question: Why four ads? Why not just one ad?

Clients often believe that ad agencies inflate ad spends so that they earn a bigger commission (those were the days of full-commission ad agency remuneration[*]). I realised that the CMD could read the four-ad campaign as a way of making UTI spend more than what it should.

I explained that if he ran one ad, it would not get noticed. It would be better if he did not run any ad at all. I gave the analogy of a ship in the night which nobody notices. By making the 'no-ad' recommendation, I believed I had more or less said 'bye bye' to a new client and a small billing.

---

[*] Till the early 2000s almost all advertising agencies were paid full media commission; 12.5 per cent to the creative agency and 2.5 per cent to the media agency. Today, agencies operate on fixed fee with a variable that is an incentive for good performance.

But my answer had a ring of truth to it and it worked. The CMD said he agreed that there was nothing like a half-pregnant (or one-fourth pregnant) woman.

We were told that he would meet us in seven days. I was naïve, or foolish enough to ask Mr Damodaran, if he would really meet us after a week.

Mr Damodaran was patient in his reply. He said he was heading to Delhi to work out the restructuring dynamics of the company and also to ask for funds for marketing. He said honestly that he had no budget, but believed in the need to do the advertising, as 'air cover' as the troops went out to manage agents and investors.

Again, Kinjal and I confabulated on what might happen. My bias quotient on UTI had come down a bit, but not totally. Kinjal of course was fully charged to execute the campaign.

I need not have worried. At the next meeting, held exactly seven days later, Mr Damodaran okayed the plan and the campaign rolled out a fortnight later. Unlike many other so-called professional companies that cut, cancel and change their advertising plans, the UTI Country campaign ran as planned.

UTI went on to escape the death trap. The team at UTI did an admirable job in keeping the flock together. A year later a new paper, while reviewing the first year of Mr Damodaran's leadership at UTI, headlined the article, 'UTI Country is Happy Again', or words to that effect. It was a happy moment for us to see that our line had gone beyond the confines of an ad.

Mr Damodaran moved to IDBI soon after and we were fortunate enough to work with him again, this time on the rebranding of Industrial Development Bank of India to IDBI with its orange and green logo. This campaign and logo change happened exactly to plan. No chopping and churning. No last-minute changes.

So was Mr Damodaran the only exception in my long years of trying to work with PSUs?

Not really. A few years after the IDBI identity and brand launch, we had the opportunity of working with Mr T. S. Vijayan who was the CMD of the Life Insurance Corporation of India (LIC). We had been trying to get the corporation to move to a more modern identity (you probably see a constant refrain in these stories), but were about to give up hope. Mr Vijayan had taken over as CMD and when asked for time his office was quick to respond and give me an appointment for the following week. I made a short presentation to explain the logic behind the new identity and the need for the same. He started by saying, 'I thought this was approved?' When I demurred, and explained that we had tested the logo, printed it in various sizes in various substrata, but there was no closure, he asked us to leave everything with him. It was now his job to make it happen.

Again, my bias crept in. But a week later, LIC called to tell us that we had the mandate to roll out the new identity campaign.

When in a sales-related function, we often develop biases towards certain types of customers. And these biases tend to cloud our thinking. I was fortunate that Kinjal Medh pushed me into committing to going the whole hog on the UTI pitch. And it opened my eyes to the new wave blowing through PSUs of India.

As I write this piece in 2018, I am convinced that some of the PSUs of India are better run than many private sector companies and I would submit, even some multinational organisations. Yes, doing business with PSUs calls for some special strengths. For one we need to keep our biases aside. And be ready to meet some amazingly insightful leaders who run India's PSUs.

I was fortunate to have met some of them. If you keep your biases aside, you may too.

A New Business Pitch That Wasn't Quite ...

In 1989, I moved to Chennai to set up Ulka Advertising's office in that city. Strange as it may sound, the agency by then already had offices in Kochi, Bangalore and Hyderabad (two had never made profits in their history), but not yet in Chennai till I was sent there to open one. While it was nice to be based out of Chennai, I travelled more than four days a week. Also, at that point, I hadn't yet pitched for any business in Chennai itself.

On one of my trips I bumped into an old friend—Chinnen Das—who asked me what I was doing in Chennai. As I explained my tryst with travel, he asked me why I wasn't yet looking for business in Chennai. I had to explain that I ran a one-man office and wasn't sure who would trust me against the many well entrenched full-fledged agencies in Chennai. But Chinnen being Chinnen, insisted that I had to meet this 'great chap' who had moved to Chennai to handle the RPG Group's business interests in the city, especially Spencer's department store.

Cut to the bar at Connemara Hotel. I met Chinnen at the promised time of 7.30 p.m. and soon we were joined by

Mr Pradipta Mohapatra, the President of Spencer's. Chinnen left soon after and I was left to work my charm on Pradipta.

I did not have to try. We spoke of many things including life in Kolkata (and my two years at Joka, where the IIM was located), the RPG Group's plans in Chennai, Ulka's old history with Ceat Tyres, another RPG Group company and so on. As the evening progressed I discovered that I was thoroughly enjoying Pradipta's company. There was so much to learn from him and his views on life. We did not speak a word about advertising or marketing. I did not ask for business, and that worked in my favour. As we ended the evening, Pradipta asked me if I would like to work on his new business plans. I confessed that I was a one-man show in Chennai and I did not want to take on his work and disappoint him. To which Pradipta replied that he was also working with a small team and where would he get a guy like me to work hands-on. As if that weren't enough, he then went on to say that he liked me, I seemed to be a good guy and that Ulka was a known agency, which had done work for the Group. And then he cut to the chase, asking me to meet him the next day.

We shook hands at 9 p.m. and that's how I landed my first account in Chennai—without any RFP, pitch or extended negotiations on team size and revenues!

I realised then that Pradipta had a tremendous ability to gauge a person, evaluate a person's worth and build a bond. While he did most of the talking at that first meeting, somewhere deep inside he was also probably judging me and forming an impression.

As I worked for the next five years on the various plans of Spencer's, I realised that Pradipta had the ability to build strong teams. And keep them motivated.

It was through him that I discovered that Harvard Business School runs a ten-week programme called the Advanced Management Program (AMP). He had attended the programme and called me to his office to share stories about AMP with me.

Later, I discovered that Pradipta was also an avid watch collector, or a horologist as they are known. So much so that Titan Watches often called him in as an advisor, to give them counsel about higher-end watch design.

Pradipta did nothing in small measure. Later, he set up the Coaching Foundation of India along with Ganesh Chella and R. Ramraj. This has become the foremost Coaching Certification Institution in India.

As I was transitioning out of my role as Advisor, FCB Ulka Advertising to a Brand Coach/Consultant, a dear friend K. Dasaratharaman (Dash) advised me that I ought to get myself certified as a CEO Coach at CFI: 'Ambi,' he said, 'you know Pradipta well, call him and go and meet him, man!' I messaged Pradipta the next day and he messaged back that he would be in Mumbai the next month and would meet me.

I forgot about this interaction and once again remembered Pradipta when I was in Chennai that December (Music Season, you see!). I called him and he asked me if I could meet him at his home the next day in the morning. When I walked in I was in for a shock. I had always seen Pradipta in the best of clothes, wearing a premium watch and more. Here was Pradipta, significantly bald, dressed in a frayed t-shirt and shorts, looking like a pale imitation of his old self. I did not know, till I walked in, that he was undergoing chemotherapy treatment. He was nonchalant, asked me to sit down, ordered a cup of tea for me and told me that he was beating the Big C and would be back to travelling in a few weeks.

Pradipta, as always, wanted me to tell him what I was planning to do. I enumerated the various things I was planning to do and Pradipta told me with a twinkle in his eye, 'Whatever you do, Ambi, don't start a business school.' I knew he had tried his hand at starting a business school in Chennai and did not want me to fall into the same trap. But he said it with a lot of candour and humour.

We got speaking about the Coaching Foundation of India and his passion for CEO Coaching. He suggested that I should do the certificate programme, but I ought to first speak with R. Sridhar in Mumbai to find out how the Coaching Certification could help me in my Brand Consulting practice.

I took his advice and enrolled for the programme that started in August 2016. We were fortunate that Pradipta had recovered well and was ready to welcome the new batch of CEO Coaches to the Induction programme. He regaled us with wonderful stories filled with life-lessons.

As I was completing my certification process, I was looking forward to reconnecting with Pradipta and continue the old dialogues we used to have. But that was not to be. Pradipta lost his fight against the Big C and passed away on 13 March 2017.

When we held a condolence meeting in memory of Pradipta Mohapatra in Mumbai and we had a room full of seasoned CEO Coaches, all whom had been certified by CFI, I realised that I was the person who had known him for the longest period. So I was asked to speak first. What I have recollected in this chapter was what I shared with the people in the room. Each of them had a similar story to tell about Pradipta, and how he managed to connect with every one of them, in some unique way.

Pradipta was a CEO of a large company. But he was a very different kind of a CEO.

There are many types of personality tests and the one that is the most commonly used is the 'Myers–Briggs Type Indicator' (MBTI). The MBTI was constructed by Katharine Cook Briggs and her daughter Isabel Briggs Myers. It is based on the typological theory proposed by Carl Jung, who had speculated that there are four principal psychological functions through which humans experience the world—sensation, intuition, feeling, and thinking—and that one of these four functions is dominant for a person most of the time. The MBTI was constructed for normal populations and emphasises the value of naturally occurring differences. The underlying assumption of the MBTI is that we all have specific preferences in the way we construe our experiences, and these preferences underlie our interests, needs, values, and motivations.

Under the MBTI, people are categorised into various groups based on:

- Outward or Inward focus (Extroversion/Introversion)
- How you take in information (Sensing/Intuition)
- How you prefer to make decisions (Thinking/Feeling)
- How you prefer to live your outer life (Judging/Perceiving)

There are short codes for various personality types such as ENTJ (Extroversion / Intuition/ Thinking / Judging). Most senior managers have highly developed Extroversion, Sensing, Thinking and Judging orientation. They depend on data and are very left-brained in their analysis (while a lot of brain research is still going on as our brain is the most complicated computer, it is believed that our left brain deals with rational elements and our right brain deals with creative and emotional elements).

I would submit that Pradipta must have been an ENFP (Extroversion / Intuition / Feeling / Perceiving) kind of a person. He was a great storyteller, speaker and extrovert. But he was also great at coming to decisions based on his intuition (giving me business in Chennai without a formal pitch, for instance). He was also a lover of art and the finer things of life. Possibly a result of his highly-tuned Feeling and Perceiving skills.*

---

* Readers may want to test their own MBTI Scores from any popular free-to-use survey available on the web. But please note, these are not authorised by the MBTI authorities and may not be accurate. There are also some strong criticism of the MBTI process, so please don't use it indiscriminately.

Clients like Pradipta are indeed rare. You learn a lot from them by just listening. You also realise that as you select your partner companies, it is most important to create a personal bond with the key individual. It is all well and good to say that it is a company-to-company relationship, but without the key glue between people on both sides, the relationship is not going to last.

I remembered the way Pradipta trusted me and many times in my own career how I have trusted service providers after spending just a couple of hours chatting with them. In hindsight, I think the calls I made based on intuition and feeling worked better than calls that were made based on sensing and thinking, hard facts and proof of concept. The usual disclaimers apply!

The Story Behind
The Logo

Among other things, Ulka has a great legacy of creating iconic logos. R. K. Joshi, one of the six people whom founder Bal Mundkur hired when he started Ulka in 1961 went on to not only create new logos, but also new typographic trends. *The Hindustan Times* (September 10, 2017) had this to day about the late R. K. Joshi: 'Font Designer—born in 1936, the late designer was a calligrapher, poet and researcher too. He created the Punjab National Bank (PNB) symbol in Gurmukhi script and that of WelcomGroup and Indian Post. He created the software (Vinyas) to create type-faces in Indian languages. In 1984, he joined the IDC (Industrial Design Centre at IIT Bombay) as professor.'

This story relates to one of his logos and how a client remembered the story behind the logo.

I was asked to fly down to Hyderabad to meet with Bhadrachalam Paperboards, a client of ours. The Hyderabad operations of the agency hinged on our relationship with ITC-owned Bhadrachalam Paperboards, a relationship we had managed to revive in the early '90s after many years of pursuit. At the Hyderabad meeting we were told that with the wind of liberalisation blowing through the country, the Monopolies and Restrictive Trade Practices Act (MRTP) was on its way out. Hence, ITC was thinking of bringing its own name into the name of Bhadrachalam Paperboards Ltd.

For the benefit of young readers, let me explain that in the '70s and '80s companies that fell under the ambit of MRTP were restricted from entering new businesses. Hence, ITC set up Bhadrachalam Paperboards Ltd. in the erstwhile state of Andhra Pradesh, at an arm's length. While one of the major shareholders of the company was ITC, the relationship in terms of branding was kept a little distant. Many multinationals and Indian companies had to resort to this kind of tap-dancing to comply with the complicated laws of the land.

Bhadrachalam Paperboards was one of the pioneers in the paperboard industry in India. It not only manufactured high-class packaging boards and paper, it was also backward integrated and grew its own pulp-producing trees. ITC had perfected the art of backward integration. They had the Indian Leaf Tobacco Division that helped farmers grow high yielding tobacco. They had a packaging and printing operation in Chennai that produced all the carton packs for their cigarettes.

The wave of liberalisation meant that ITC could one day integrate all its various subsidiaries into the mother ship, ITC Ltd. It wanted to make a beginning by figuring out what to do with the Hyderabad-based company's name.

The client who met me at Hyderabad was quite open about the brief. He explained that the company was wondering if they ought to drop the Bhadrachalam name itself and instead opt for a name like ITC Paperboards. They were also open to seeing if ITC could be added to the name of the company: ITC Bhadrachalam Paperboards Ltd., for instance.

ITC had always had deep enduring relationships with its advertising and marketing research partners. This is a long tradition and goes back to the '60s. I knew the story, or should I say legend, of how Mr Ajit Narain Haksar had spent time with Bhaskar Mundkur who was then the Marketing Research Manager at Lever Bros and how they developed an enduring friendship. So when Mr. Haksar became the Member-Marketing at ITC (Director-Marketing in today's parlance), and when Bhaskar Mundkur became the Managing Director of his brother's agency, Ulka, the relationship was revived. Ulka got the opportunity to work on campaigns that became legendary, like the first corporate campaign for ITC. The agency was never seen as a vendor and was always treated as a partner, both in the office and in the evenings at the graceful parties ITC managers hosted for their agency friends.

Back to our ITC Bhadrachalam story, I was asked what the agency would recommend. And I was to meet the incoming Chairman of ITC, Mr K. L. Chugh in Delhi the following Monday.

We were not sure if the double-barrel logo would be easy to use in marketing communications. While ITC is a short name, Bhadrachalam was a long one as names go. Having two names joined at the hip could lead to the company being referred to as either one of the two and the purpose of adding 'ITC' could be lost, given the length of the other name. But we knew that the name Bhadrachalam had a lot going for it.

The city of Bhadrachalam is one of the holy cities of Andhra Pradesh. Situated on the river Godavari, the city's Bhadrachalam temple for Lord Rama dated back to the seventeenth century. The city was the birth place of the poet Bhadrachala Ramadas, who lived in the seventeenth century and is one of the most famous Telugu composers along with Saint Tyagaraya, Annamacharya and Shyma Shastri. So the name Bhadrachalam held a lot of significance. We were not sure if we ought to drop the name altogether from the name of the company. But adding ITC to an existing long company name was also not sounding to be too good an option.

My trip back to Bangalore got me thinking and after brainstorming with the team it was felt that we should show the client all the options but strongly push for a double-barrel name. Our escape route was that this double-barrel name could become shorter in five years after it was clearly established that ITC Bhadrachalam Paperboards Ltd. was an ITC company. At that stage the paper and paperboard could carry the brand name Bhadrachalam, so that the holy and well-regarded name stayed alive. The master designer at our Bangalore office, Uday Parkar, created a terrific looking ad that used a visual of paper rolls and played on that to show how the company was progressing. Interestingly we created only one ad to be taken to the Chairman. But we played with various options on the placement of the brand name. ITC Paperboards Ltd., ITC Bhadrachalam Paperboards Ltd., Bhadrachalam ITC Paperboards Ltd. were the options considered. We also created options where the ITC name was provided below the Bhadrachalam name and the company was branded an 'ITC Group Company'.

In Delhi the next Monday I was asked to meet Mr K. L. Chugh at the ITC Maurya hotel. The meeting started at 8 p.m. and it was a one-on-one meeting. Mr Chugh knew the founders of the agency and asked after their health and well-being. He then sought the agency's opinion on what the name transition should be. I explained the need to continue the link to Bhadrachalam and the idea that we should simply attach the ITC name to Bhadrachalam Paperboard Ltd.'s name. Mr Chugh commented that he too felt that way and wanted to look at how the agency proposed to announce this to the public.

The single ad I had carried worked like a charm. He cleared the ad and then we got talking. He asked me if I knew of the history of the Bhadrachalam logo. I had done some reading up on the logo and how it had been created by R. K. Joshi. I knew that it used the combination of the Telugu letter 'Ba' with the English letter 'B'. It was also designed to look like a box, the product that is made from the paperboard manufactured by the company. Mr Chugh felt my knowledge was not sufficient. Then over the next thirty minutes he explained how the logo was a master design. He pointed out how the logo had multiple corners and this particular logo was designed to indicate that the paperboard manufactured by BPL could take multiple folds. This was to make an important point. In paperboard packaging, the usual problem is that paper tends to tear at the edges, but the logo seemed to indicate that Bhadrachalam paperboards products wouldn't tear at the edges. There were many more points Mr Chugh remembered about the logo. I was quite fascinated how the Chairman of a large company like ITC could remember all these minute details.

I was then requested to meet the outgoing Chairman of ITC, Mr J. N. Sapru at the ITC Guest House in Lutyens' Delhi the next morning. I joined Mr Sapru for breakfast and presented the logo thoughts and the print ad to the Chairman as he was munching on buttered toast. The meeting, unlike the one with Mr Chugh lasted all of twenty minutes. Mr Sapru asked me what the agency thought and I reiterated the need to retain the Bhadrachalam name. He agreed. He then asked me to show him the ad, took one look and said it was good to go. The meeting was over and I was on my way back to the Ulka Delhi office.

It was my good fortune that at the Delhi office, Arvind Wable, after listening to my tales of ITC Bhadrachalam, suggested that we meet Ann Mukherjee, Bal Mundkur's partner when he had founded Ulka in 1961. I readily agreed and we were fortunate that Ann was in the office that morning. I narrated the complete story to her and told her how I got a lesson on logo design from the Chairman of ITC, Mr K. L. Chugh. Ann laughed and said that was the power of a great story.

Apparently when the agency presented the logo of the yet-to-be formed Bhadrachalam Paperboards, many years ago, Mr Chugh was part of the team that approved the logo. Ann explained how the 'Ba' logo was presented with more than 100 charts, which demonstrated the logic behind the logo. She did not remember the 'Box' or the 'Perfect Corner' rationale, but felt that the agency had built a great story around the logo and the logo presentation had lasted well over three hours.

In the book *The Power of Story*, Jim Loehr speaks of how stories should have in them a purpose, a truth and a lot of hope-filled action. As we migrate from an old story to a new story, we need to ensure that the new story has purpose, truth and action. The new story has to be embedded through writing and rewriting, through thinking and visualising and through talking and acting. Finally, new stories have to become part of a new ritual.

The case of the Bhadrachalam logo is one such story that ended up becoming so powerful that the Chairman remembered it along with its many elements twenty years after it was first presented. What was also fascinating to me was the easy way in which an advertising executive, and forget the titles for the moment, could sit and chat with the Chairmen (incoming and outgoing) with such easy candour. What was also revealing to me was the fact that both Mr Chugh and Mr Sapru were open to hearing what the agency team thought of the name change. Our brief was quite open and we had the liberty to suggest a totally new name. But finally what we suggested found favour or you might say that we reflected the internal thinking of the company. Be that as it may, the entire process that was played out in under five days was truly memorable. I got a lesson on the power of a logo, the power of a story, from no less a person than the Chairman of one of India's most respected companies. Could I ask for more?

An Apple A Day

As a young client service executive in advertising, my wish for a dream account was fulfilled rather early. The agency, Rediffusion Advertising, was called to handle the launch of a new product by Cadbury India. I trooped along with the big honchos for the first meeting and that was when I first met Vinita Bali. She was the Group Product Manager at Cadbury, an alumnus of Jamnalal Bajaj School of Management and I think this was her second job. Her boss, the Marketing Manager was Deepak Shourie, a marketing veteran who would later go on to launch *Outlook* magazine.

The briefing meeting was a rather short one. We were told the various reasons behind the new product launch (an apple juice-based drink) by Cadbury India and we were to handle the launch of this new product, the first that Cadbury was launching in the country outside its core product range of chocolates. I suspect there was some government nudging that prompted them to get into an agro-based product, a product that had its raw materials sourced from the northernmost parts of India.

I was given a free hand to work on the preliminary information-gathering and competitive strategy for the brand. As a part of my due diligence I expanded the competitive set to not just include traditional bottled soft drinks such as Thums Up, Gold Spot,

Limca, Campa Cola but also products such as fruit squashes (Kissan), soft drink concentrates (Rasna) and other beverages like Rooh Afza. After examining the label declaration of all these products/brands (over twenty of them, I think), I then analysed the advertising for each of these brands, then the merchandising (there was no shortcut like a website to look at those days). I managed to bring some method to the madness by creating a large template that captured all the brands and the multifarious benefits offered by them. In order to capture all this in one place, I went and bought what was then called 'double foolscap' paper and created by hand, a large spreadsheet of sorts.

The competition review presentation to Deepak Shourie and Vinita Bali happened a couple of weeks after the first meeting. I thought the meeting went well. I was particularly thrilled when Vinita complimented me on the 'Benefit Matrix' I had created on the foolscap paper. I think she even asked me for a copy of the same.

Remember, I was the lowest in the food chain and here was one of the most respected marketing companies seeking my template. I was delighted.

Then came product research. Once again, I was asked if I would like to accompany the research team, consisting of marketing research veteran the late Ramesh Thadani, and Vinita Bali to various cities where the research (elaborate product tests and consumer interviews) were happening. I readily agreed and convinced my boss to let me go for ten days. It was a great learning experience, once again.

Post-research, the brand strategy was jointly worked out between the agency and the client. The brand, which had by then got a brand name—'Appela'—was to be positioned as a 'natural refreshing drink', since it was made from apple juice and had no additives. The tag line was 'Refreshing Return To Nature'. Since

I was almost an integral part of the brand planning process, the agency generously asked me to make the final presentation to the client.

The campaign consisted of five television commercials each of them presenting a typical consumer or intended consumer of Appela. Each of these interesting characters had a 'nickname' and my presentation started with a story about my nickname, 'Ambi'. The campaign virtually sold itself.

I worked on the campaign production, but then left Rediffusion to join Boots as a Product Manager in early 1982. The brand Appela was launched in mid-1982 and the campaign created a huge wave, including winning the 'Campaign of the Year' Award from Advertising Club Bombay. Unfortunately, the brand did not meet up to the expectations of the company and had to be withdrawn a year later.

I missed working on the final product roll-out but heard that Vinita was often spotted riding with the delivery vans making their routes across crowded Mumbai. I would have enjoyed learning the finer art of selling to the trade from her.

When I met Vinita Bali three years later at an industry event, we chatted about what could have saved Appela. Vinita observed that if we had launched it in a tetrapak (Frooti had just been launched in a tetrapak) may be Appela could have succeeded. Looking back today, I even wonder if the current success of Paper Boat may also have been, in some measure, due to its unique packaging format.

Working with Vinita I realised that she did not treat me like a lowly account executive from an agency, but virtually as an integral member of the marketing team. I suspect she was behind Deepak Shourie's move to try and hire me into Cadbury's brand team in 1986. I was then struggling with housing issues in Mumbai and if only Cadbury had offered me housing, I probably would have jumped from Boots to Cadbury. As it turned out, it was Boots that offered me housing and I stayed behind to sell Sweetex, Coldarin and Brufen for two more years.

I was lucky that early in my career I got to work on a huge consumer product launch. I think I was doubly lucky that in Vinita Bali I had a mentor, someone who was ready to counsel and mentor a young colleague. As I moved to marketing I hope I carried some of those characteristics into my new job. Fortunately, I worked with three terrific agencies in my tenure at Boots: HTA (now JWT), Clarion and Trikaya. I think I made some very good friends in each of those agencies. I even helped some of them find new jobs and happily fought battles on their behalf with ad film makers and models.

In my long career of four decades I have had the opportunity to interact with many woman managers but I still remember Vinita Bali for her support and the very polite way in which she boosted my confidence. No wonder she was handpicked by Coca Cola USA after a stellar career spanning fourteen years with Cadbury. She later returned to India to head Britannia, the biscuit and cookie major. In 2009, she founded the Britannia Nutrition Foundation which combats child malnutrition through the distribution of fortified biscuits to Indian schoolchildren. She won a Corporate Social Responsibility Award for her work with the foundation. In 2011, *Forbes* named her on its list of 'Asia's 50 Power Businesswomen'. Vinita is also the Chair of the Board of the Directors of the Global Alliance for Improved Nutrition (GAIN).

Speaking about successful women executives, Rama Bijapurkar, one of India's most respected strategy consultants (and her late husband Ashok Bijapurkar) has been a constant source of support and counsel, both in my book writing adventures as well as on the kind of office I should set up as an independent brand strategy consultant.

In FCB Ulka too, we were very fortunate to have some truly amazing women executives, some of whom went on to achieve great success in the agency group and some who went on to head large organisations. At one time three of my five direct reports were women.

It is fashionable to speak about gender diversity today, but what did we do that helped us achieve the miracle more than two decades ago?

For one we recruited a large number of MBAs from the leading business schools. Shashi Sinha ran this for a decade and then handed it over to Savita Mathai, yet another first day recruit into FCB Ulka from Narsee Monjee Institute of Management Studies. We used to get a large number of women applicants from business schools. For one, FCB Ulka was seen as a good clean organisation to work and learn in. Secondly, it had an MBA culture. Thirdly, I think advertising was seen as a slightly softer sector to work in, compared to hard-core consumer marketing (riding trucks in cities is not every woman's dream job).

We did get a number of women joining, but how did we manage to retain them? Anil Kapoor, the Chairman and Shashi Sinha figured out that the way to help women stay in the job is to be liberal with the maternity leave options. The company offered three months maternity leave but thereafter the company was ready to offer a flexi-time schedule to the women who did not have good baby care at home. So someone could opt to work just three-and-a-half days a week for six months before coming back to full-time employment. But by bridging the challenges of women in a largely patriarchal Indian society, we managed to retain a number of highly talented women.

To be fair the Indian marketing research industry had also adopted this method to retain the best women. I would submit they too benefited immensely from this flexible HR policy.

Coming back to my learnings from my client, I think working with Vinita Bali on the Appela launch was very satisfying. More satisfying was to be treated as an equal. Something that is not seen too often in the world of client-agency relationships.

On my return from my long Appela reseach trips, Arun Kale, the Creative Director at the agency asked me, 'What is all this management/MBA about? What do you fellows learn in your MBA course? Why should you be paid so well?' I remembered to pick up a book for him on my next trip. The book I picked up for him was *Practice of Management* by Peter Drucker.

I had read it as a part of my MBA course and found it simple, yet highly insightful. Thankfully he too agreed after reading it, that it was a great primer to what goes by the name 'management'.

Some of the key points raised by Peter Drucker include: neither results nor resources exist inside the business (roping in an agency team member as your own therefore makes great sense); any leadership position is transitory and likely to be short-lived (a client today can be an agency person tomorrow); results are obtained by exploiting opportunities, not by solving problems; resources to produce results should be allocated to opportunities; economic results are earned only by leadership.

Working with clients who treated you with respect and regard made me a better professional. A confident one too. It made me realise that as a client, the agency, and as an agency person—the film producer, the photographer and the event manager, are all part of your large apple garden. They can all help you get the right nutrition to deliver on your objectives.

A Giant Learns
to Dance*

It would not be an exaggeration to say that Tata Consultancy Services (TCS) virtually created the Indian ITES (Information Technology Enabled Services) industry. But as per Tata traditions it had always maintained a low profile. Its founding CEO or Director-in-Charge as he was titled, Mr F. C. Kohli was very media shy and the company had almost no presence in media reports. The fact that it was a division of the unlisted Tata Sons did not help either. While its publicly listed competitors got written about every quarter, TCS hardly found a mention.

ITES is a rather short abbreviation for a lot of things that these companies do. Their range of services include application development and maintenance, quality assurance testing, migration and reengineering, enterprise portals and content management, business intelligence and data warehousing and e-business solutions. Indian ITES companies had their big bang moment with the scare around Y2K in the years leading to 2000.

---

* The title of this chapter is inspired by former IBM CEO Lou Gerstner's book, *Who Says Elephants Can't Dance.*

Global companies were worried that all their computers would crash as the clock turned to 00.01 a.m. on January 1, 2000. In fact predictions were so dire that there was fear of aircrafts falling off the sky, power grids shutting down, telecom networks crashing and of course, the internet going off in a big bang.

The global Y2K fear drove up the demand for ITES offerings and Indian companies were very well-positioned to take care of the global surge in demand for trained IT folks. TCS led the charge and managed to keep its competitors at bay.

Soon after the Y2K moment, we started hearing murmurs about TCS going in for a public listing with an Initial Public Offering (IPO). As the agency on record we were called to start thinking about what the campaign should be like.

In the mid-nineties, the terrain for Indian ITES companies was changing rapidly. It was the prevalent feeling that global majors like Accenture and IBM Global Services would soon set up offices in India and destroy the wage arbitrage that Indian companies enjoyed. There was also a fear that as compared to a 'services' company like TCS, a company like Accenture brought with it a strong 'consulting' aura. At such a juncture, there were a lot of things in the air at TCS. The feeling was that Tata Consultancy Services was too long a name and it did not communicate the right values. There were doubts about using what some felt was an archaic term like 'Consultancy' and the feeling of 'being shackled' to the term 'Services'. Then there were questions about whether the parent company brand Tata, with its salt to steel old-world bias, was adding or detracting from the company's core offering in information technology.

At this point in 1996, Mr Subramanian Ramadorai, popularly known as S. Ramadorai or Ram to friends, took over the role of CEO of TCS in the year 1996. Under his leadership the company managed to reap huge gains during the Y2K boom.

But Mr Ramadorai was on the job of transforming the company from one that was depending on sending IT professionals to the US and enjoying a wage arbitrage, into a company that would fully harness the power of remote working. He was also pushing the company into changing its ways of working, from that of negotiating on the basis of the lowest price to discussing the concept of what value TCS could add to the operations of any client they partnered with.

It was around the early 2000s that there were reports in the media that the numero uno position of TCS was under threat from its most media-savvy competitor. The suggestions that were floated included changing the name of the company, to dropping the term 'services' from the name.

I had the opportunity to sit in on some of these heated discussions. And it was a learning experience to see how Mr Ramadorai would tackle the issues that were thrown at him, in his own soft-spoken seemingly unassertive manner. I remember him once saying, 'Our company is in the business of providing a service, how can we drop that from our title. Yes, our name may be a lot less simple than that of our competitors, but we will live with it.' He had set the company on a major transformation journey, from being one of the top twenty or thirty ITES firms into being in the top ten Global IT Services companies in a decade.

Note the way the plans were made. This was a man in a hurry, but he was not in such a hurry as to damage the fabric of the company, so painstakingly built over three decades. He wanted change, but it had to happen in a steady manner.

While working on the advertising campaign for the IPO, the team at the agency was tasked to create a campaign that extolled the achievements of the company. We knew that a public issue had been on the cards for many years, but as always, the agency got only a few weeks to create the campaign.

The ads focused on the key achievements of TCS. Some of the lines used in the ads were:

'IT put India on the world map. But who put "IT" on the Indian map?' (This was intended to communicate that TCS had pioneered the Indian IT software and services industry.)

'When does the day end when you are working around the clock, around the world?' (Here, we were attempting to establish that TCS had pioneered the global delivery model.)

'Money makes the world go round. But who makes the money go around?' (This was to highlight TCS's core strengths in financial services software segment and more.)

'Do you ever think of software saving lives?' (Here, it was about communicating how TCS was investing in research in the critical area of healthcare.)

All the ads spoke about TCS's heritage: 'We have been, and are, the leading Indian IT services company with over 28,000 employees of 30 nationalities, providing solutions to clients in 32 countries. If that is not global, what is? TCS Truly Global.'

The four-ad print campaign ran in the leading newspapers and it was for the first time TCS was coming out with its story, in mass media, in glorious colour. The ads went through the usual approval process, but given the paucity of time, the approvals came rather fast.

I am sure Mr Ramadorai asked a lot of questions and needed a lot of convincing by his team on the need for four full-page colour ads in newspapers. But he gave his approval and the ads ran.

Anecdotally, the campaign did a world of good for the company. Companies tend to dismiss the power of corporate campaigns. But it has been proven that the biggest impact a corporate campaign has is on its own people. And we did hear that the TCS folks started to feel a few inches taller after seeing the campaign in the leading dailies and magazines.

The TCS IPO opened when the market was not really at its bullish best. But still, the issue was oversubscribed 7.7 times. The TCS scrip was listed on the Bombay Stock Exchange and National Stock Exchange on Wednesday, 25 August 2004. The transformation of TCS from a division of Tata Sons to a publicly-listed company was complete and it had been achieved in a very calm and sedate manner by the CEO, Mr S. Ramadorai. But it was a transformation indeed, and I was fortunate to be an observer of this transformation. Obviously, as an advertising and marketing services partner, my visibility into all the changes that were taking place in TCS was limited. But since I did know almost all the senior executives of the company, I knew the changes that were happening were dramatic.

Little wonder that Mr Ramadorai was awarded the 'Padma Bhushan' by the government of India in 2006. When he handed the company over to his successor Mr N. Chandrasekaran, it was not the same company that Mr Kohli had handed over to him. And true to form, Mr Chandrasekaran took the company to even greater heights, before moving on to become the Chairman of Tata Sons.

Prof. John Kotter of Harvard Business School has been studying organisational transformation for decades. He has found that most change initiatives, whether to boost quality, or improve culture or reverse a death spiral, generate only lukewarm results. In fact, most fail miserably.

Prof. Kotter has found the key reason and has presented this in his book *Leading Change*. It is not as if managers don't know the importance of transformation. But they tend to see it as an event, as a big bang. The reality is that transformation is not an event but a process. Transformation has to be undertaken in stages as each stage feeds into the next and so on. Often CEOs fall into the trap of hurrying through the change process, by dramatic announcements and replacement of key generals. Equally disturbing is the tendency of CEOs to declare victory too early. These grand declarations end up reversing hard-won gains and can devastate the process. Truly successful CEOs on the other hand, understand the various stages, the pitfalls in each stage and never lose focus on the end goal.

Prof. Kotter has enumerated eight steps to be performed to achieve total transformation:

- Establishing a sense of urgency
- Forming a powerful guiding coalition
- Creating a vision
- Communicating the vision
- Empowering others to act on the vision
- Planning for and creating short-term wins
- Consolidating improvements and producing still more change
- Institutionalising new approaches

I cannot say that I was able to observe all these eight stages playing out as TCS was transformed, but I know that many of these things happened, in a calm and steady manner. I believe that anyone in a client-facing situation in marketing services, in financial services or any other service, can learn a lot by observing how organisations are transformed by leaders. And take those lessons to their own organisations.

As Prof. Kotter says, 'By understanding the stages of change—and the pitfalls unique to each stage—you boost your chances of a successful transformation. The payoff? Your organisation flexes with tectonic shifts in competitors, markets, and technology—leaving rivals far behind.'

As managers and leaders, we are tasked with transforming the organisations we run and we can make the mistake of jumping headlong into a big bang transformation and change initiative. And fail.

Listening and learning from the transformation at TCS, I could see how transformation is not a 'big bang' but a gradual process, nudged along by a visionary leader, with the help of a core team that believes in this vision, with clear short-term goals (the IPO, for instance), and finally, institutionalisation of transformation initiatives.

To read more about the TCS journey, you should delve into Mr Ramadorai's book *The TCS Story & Beyond*.

Failing to Try
Versus Failing

As a marketing services provider, besides interacting with some of the top corporate leaders of the country, I have also had the opportunity to interact with a whole variety of entrepreneurs. And many of them taught me valuable lessons. But let me start with a story I heard from FCB Ulka Delhi's CEO, Arvind Wable.

The agency had been briefed by a company called InfoEdge which had a job site called naukri.com. The founder of the company, Sanjiv Bikchandani wanted to ensure that his job site did not just offer 'naukris' to the lowest end of the corporate hiring spectrum. He had raised funds and it was clear that unless he dramatically improved the quality of CVs on his site, he would not be able to attract high-value clients (corporates who post jobs, for a fee, on a jobsite) to his site. And if he did not get good job listings, he would not attract good CVs. So it was the proverbial chicken and egg problem.

The agency team had done a lot of research but it was qualitative consumer insight mining that led to the creative breakthrough. The film they presented to Sanjiv and team went something like this:

It is the executive washroom. The younger staff are washing their hands and they spot the boss coming in and move aside to give him space. The suit-clad balding boss washes his hands and then spots the guy whom he is really angry with. He begins lambasting him right there in the washroom, in front of all his colleagues. As he continues, the young guy, with total chutzpah decides to go back to the wash basin to splash some water on his boss, who is taken aback at this gesture. He then smiles and walks away, much to the amazement of the boss. The screen fades to black and the copy fades in. 'Guess who has heard from us?' the last frame flashes and then, it reads 'Naukri.com. India's No. 1 Jobsite.'

There was no audio mention of the brand name naukri.com. In fact, the brand name appears only in the last three seconds of the film. If you missed the last three seconds you missed the name of the brand. There was also no mention in the ad that naukri.com had a lot of exciting jobs listed or that it was a quick way of quitting your job and finding a better one. There was no sales pitch at all.

The ad in fact, did not say much. Even the boss' tirade was inaudible. You could only make out that he was gesticulating wildly and was probably using expletives.

In many ways, it was a risky ad to run. The target audience may have missed the whole story. Or may have misunderstood the issue. The folks who post jobs, the bosses, may have got upset.

Many packaged goods companies have rules about advertising and brand mention. It is said that if the ad is of thirty seconds duration the brand name should be mentioned within the first sixteen seconds and in total, the brand should appear and should be mentioned in audio at least three times. The naukri.com 'washroom' ad violated all these tenets.

The agency buttressed its arguments by saying that consumer insight mining had revealed that the single most important reason for a young executive to quit his job was the boss. Traditional research may point to things like salary, title, industry, city, office, but the hidden reason is that the young executive hates the boss. So the ad was based on solid insight. But it was being presented to a first-time entrepreneur who was making his first foray into television advertising.

Think about it. The company had just raised funding. Was this the best way to utilise those funds?

The agency did not want to push the concept. So I am told the agency team warned the client that this was a rather risky approach. It could work brilliantly or it could fail. If it worked well, it would in all likelihood actually end up getting a lot of good quality CVs to the site and that could set in motion a positive cycle. If it bombed it would be good money down the tube (literally!), and the ad could antagonise the folks who post job requirements on the website.

Sanjiv Bikchandani thought through the options and then decided to go with this ad. But he did tell the team to keep half the budget aside to explore an alternative script if this one failed. He did not tell us to put all our money into this. He was ready to take the risk, but carefully.

The ad ended up working like a storm. The quality of CVs on the site dramatically improved, which in turn improved job postings. The 'washroom' ad was followed by the even more risky 'Hari Sadu' ad, which went on the be rated as the ad of the decade.

This is an interesting trait of entrepreneurs that Prof. Adam Grant explores in his highly readable book *Originals*. But more about this later.

Let us move to yet another entrepreneur.

Thanks to a client in Ahmedabad, I ended up visiting that city every fortnight during the late '90s. On one of those trips, I was asked by good friend and well-wisher, Sajida Sharma, to meet one Darshanbhai Patel. Darshanbhai was creating waves with highly targeted brands in the Over the Counter (OTC) medication space. His brands Moov and Krack had made a great impact. So it became a bit of a habit for me to visit him in Ahmedabad to listen to his views on brand building.

Darshanbhai took over the company Paras Phamaceuticals, a company that used to sell a headache tablet, Panjon, and transformed it into a very successful OTC player. His Moov took on the traditional leader Iodex and became the biggest-selling pain-relieving balm. His advertising focused on the aspect that a backache relieving cream need not stain your clothes (Iodex was coloured and had that potential weakness). He supported the brand with heavy duty advertising on Doordarshan (DD), often outspending his rival by a factor of three or four. After tasting success with Moov, he launched Krack. This cream was aimed at the cracks on the feet of women. Though there was no large national brand playing in this market, consumers were using a variety of remedies including Vaseline and Boroline. Once again the brand was supported through heavy duty advertising on DD. It too went on to become a big national brand. He then tried his hand with an anti-itching product, Itchguard.

When I first met Darshanbhai, he was in the thick of the launch of his hair care brand Livon. The brand was a serum that one had to 'leave on' one's hair after coming out of the bath. The product was modelled after very premium hair serum brands sold in the developed markets.

Darshanbhai was quite voluble about his tried-and-tested strategy. He launched his new brands with total domination of the national television medium. Those were the early days of cable TV, but he, however, had tremendous faith in DD. His launch was often done through heavy-duty advertising on the Hindi feature film slots on Saturdays and Sundays. His deal with the media company was that his brand should have the 'biggest' share of FCTs (Free Commercial Time) on the slot. This strategy was meticulously followed for at least six weeks and in previous launches, had worked well. But in the case of Livon he was not getting the kind of response he was used to and we spent time discussing the barriers. Mind you, I was not representing his ad agency, but he was quite okay discussing his issues with me. I admired his openness and I suspect I ended up learning a lot more from those interactions than Darshanbhai himself. He wanted me to work on a new category he was planning to enter and had promised me that range of products. But luck did not favour me and we never got to work with him. My loss. Eventually, Darshanbhai managed to bundle all his brands together and sell them for a pretty package; even the non-performer Livon ended living on under the care of a new owner.

Darshanbhai was a true marketing thinker who managed to understand the power of mass media to build OTC and consumer brands. His belief was that even cosmetic brands in India need to be sold like a medicine and he had tested this with his brands like Krack and Borosoft. He was willing to take risks with untested concepts. He was reported to be a tough and demanding client, but he also believed in long relationships with his agency partners. (Chandan Nath, an old friend was his long-serving agency partner from Mudra Ahmedabad.) He did invest in consumer research, but used his own judgement to decide the brand strategy.

Another Indian entrepreneur whom I crossed paths with was Nitish Jain. After failing in some attempts to crack the Fast Moving Consumer Goods (FMCG) market, he hit pay dirt with Captain Cook Salt. The first ads of Captain Cook Salt that focused on whiteness and purity did not work. Later, his agency Lintas managed to create a breakthrough ad using a testimonial approach where Captain Cook Salt was compared with the market leader and was positioned as 'non-sticky' and 'quick flow'. This worked wonderfully and Nitish Jain wanted to take the Captain Cook franchise to other categories.

The task of launching Captain Cook Atta came to Ulka Advertising (interestingly, for a short period Ulka, which was based in Nirmal Building in Nariman Point had clients on four or five floors of the building; Captain Cook was on floor 18, I think). The ad film that was created showed a modern, SUV-driving farmer complaining about the fussiness of the Captain Cook company and the way they bought wheat grain from him, as if they were buying gold. His wife replies that the atta is in fact, so good that he, as he was lamenting about the Captain Cook Company, had polished off so many rotis. He is surprised that she too was using Captain Cook atta.

The film was to go on air and since the brand Captain Cook Atta was to be launched in Mumbai first, the agency recommended niche English television channels; however, cautioning that the reach of these channels was limited. Nitish Jain wanted to know what would make 50 per cent of the affluent households aware of the atta offering. The only option was Hindi GEC (general entertainment channels), and the agency team cautioned on the huge wastage since only 15 to 20 per cent of the viewership was in Greater Mumbai city. Nitish Jain, the entrepreneur that he was, decided that he would like the ad to be aired on the Hindi GECs. His argument was that he had to make atta a success and national advertising would ensure the brand gets the trial it needs, but more importantly it would be seen all over the atta consuming market. In a sense, it would seed the market. This is contrarian thinking if there was one. Classical marketing thinking would have said that you should start advertising only after the product in available in the market. Here was an Indian entrepreneur who was willing to throw caution to the winds to make an impact. To complete the story, Nitish Jain ended up selling the Captain Cook brand to a global major and managed to recoup all his marketing investments and a sizable amount on top of that.

As you can see, these three stories about the creation of Indian brands, by Indian entrepreneurs does have a common theme. The enterpreneurs were willing to take risks, but they examined their options before taking their decisions.

In the book *Originals,* Prof. Adam Grant of Wharton Business School of the University of Pennsylvania, makes some interesting observations about original thinkers, and how they take actions. He says that original thinkers develop an ability to manage risks in generating, recognising and voicing original ideas. The key skill seems to be the ability to recognise ideas. They often face the dilemma of how and when to scale and many original thinkers procrastinate before jumping all in. They allow dissenting opinions to flourish and are open to new ideas. They don't hold back their emotions. Darshanbhai was quite open about his concern with the slower offtake of Livon. Nitish Jain was concerned about the muscle power of Hindustan Unilever.

To quote Prof Adam Grant, 'Ultimately, the people who choose to champion originality are the ones who propel us forward ... their inner experiences are not any different from our own. They feel the same fear, the same doubt, as the rest of us. What sets them apart is that they take action anyway. They know in their hearts that failing would yield less regret than failing to try.'

All these successful Indian entrepreneurs showed us that they had to try, and may be fail. But not trying was not an option.

Lights, Camera, Action!

There is a celebrity fever sweeping through the world of Indian advertising and marketing. In a study done by the S. P. Jain Institute of Management and Research (SPJIMR) in 2016, during the peak festival season almost 35 per cent of the ads that were aired on the heavily-watched Hindi channels featured a celebrity. In fact, only in South Korea do you have a higher percentage of advertising featuring celebrities. All other countries have a smaller percentage of celebrities in ads; even in the US, the capital of ads and celebrities, the number does not exceed 30 per cent. In Europe, it is significantly smaller. We also have to remember that the breadth of celebrities is rather narrow in India; but for the exception of a few tennis and badminton players, TV stars and yoga gurus, all the celebrities featured in Indian ads are from filmdom (Bollywood/Kollywood/Tollywood) or cricket. Hence on any given day, you may see the same film star endorsing a car, a shampoo, an underwear brand and a fairness cream, in no particular order.

So what happens behind the scenes when an Indian client signs on a celebrity to endorse a brand?

As someone who has been around for a long time, I must confess that I have been witness to and hear about all kinds of weird behavior. One story that I heard was about how a client flew down with his entire extended family from Kolkata to Mumbai so that all of them could be on the sets to watch this superstar perform, when he/she was shooting for the ad. In fact, temporary seating arrangements for the extended family (some were over sixty years of age) were constructed. And then there are the stories of how the toughest of the tough clients melt in front of celebrities and start asking for their autographs (it's now a selfie!).

But this is not such a story.

This large consumer product brand had a long history with the agency. The agency had helped the client turn around the fortunes of the brand. The brand had a consistent advertising copy platform that had evolved over a decade into a polished template. The client believed in working with trusted partners and so even the ad film maker was someone they had been working with for over seven years. Then, the following incident unfolded.

This client, for the first time in their history, decided to sign up a Bollywood celebrity and all the details had been ironed out. The talent agency had drafted the contract and it had been signed and a film was shot. The time then came for the second film to be made. The star decided to throw a tantrum. He did not like the ad film maker, for purely personal reasons and asked for a change. The agency team felt that it was unfair to dump the ad film maker who had stayed with the brand for well over seven years. The film maker, in a gracious move, offered to back off. But we knew that it would have been a bit of an embarrassment. The client was informed of the crisis.

There are some clients who can call a spade a spade.

The client called me for a quick word and asked me what the real problem was. The ad film maker was one of the most respected in the ad industry, so clearly there was something more that was not meeting the eye. I presented some hypotheses, none fully verified. The client asked me for my view. I did not want to push him towards any decision and told him to take his own decision. I assured him that we would figure out a solution, whatever happened. The film maker was a perfect gentleman and we would not upset him, if in case we decided to accede to the demands of this temperamental star. But the client was made of sterner stuff. He was convinced that he was not going to buckle.

The talent agency was summoned to the client office and the client decided to read out the riot act to the talent agency. Fortunately enough, homework had been done and it was found that the film star did not have a say on the choice of the film maker, though he had a say on the script, up to a point. The client asked the talent agency to get the film star to agree, or return the talent fees (pro rata) paid to him. They were not given an option.

I think the talent agency was relieved when the client took such a tough stand. They gave the film star no options. 'Either you show up for the shoot, or return the multi-crore advance received for the endorsement,' was the message conveyed. You can guess what happened next.

There are also several humorous stories featuring celebrities. There was one where this client had taken the agency team to present a script (for a telecom brand) to a lady film star. She threw a tantrum without even listening to the full script. Then she came up with the suggestion that the client should sack the agency that had prepared this 'lousy' script (and was sitting in the very same room) and hire the Delhi agency that had shot a 'wonderful' film with the star the previous month. The client had to point out that it was the same agency which had done the previous film, just a different office from a different city. The lady was then told that the agency has offices in Mumbai, Delhi and other cities. The lady in question then put on her best 'I am so surprised look'. With that out of the way the script narration went smoothly and the film got made.

For every story about a client standing up to a celebrity, there are probably ten where the client turns into putty in the hands of the star.

Our Hyderabad branch manager had been alerted by the head office that a tea brand wanted this very famous cricketer to endorse their new brand. Fortunately, we had a colleague in the Hyderabad office who had gone to the same college/school as this cricket star. After much negotiation the fee was agreed at a level that was almost 50 per cent lower than what was originally quoted. The critical meeting was arranged between the client CEO and the cricket star, in a five star hotel in Hyderabad. The CEO and the agency were waiting, as is always the case, and the cricketer sauntered in half an hour late. The CEO turned into jelly when he saw the star. He pulled out a card and asked the star player for his autograph gushing, 'My whole family is your big fan. This autograph is for my daughter!' The cricketer's advisor who was with him quickly revised the endorsement fees to the pre-negotiated level. The deal got signed, with the CEO not wanting to be seen as churlish and petty.

These are just a few stories from both sides of the fence. Clients often do not realise that the celebrities are also in awe of them, the size of their companies, the financial muscle, the thousands of people who work for the company and so on. I am sure if the CEO mentioned above had taken five minutes to explain to the star the size and scope of the company and the brand, the potential future deals, the negotiations would have gone the other way. I am not for a minute saying that all celebrities are equally difficult or opinionated. Some of the biggest names are the most humble when it comes to working on advertisements. The onus is on the client to decide where to draw the line.

When a client is ready to stand up to bullying, you realise that there is a better way of doing this.

What could be the lessons in these stories?

In his book *The Halo Effect*, Prof. Phil Rosenzweig looks at pseudoscientific tendencies to explain business success. He identifies nine, what he calls 'delusions' that cloud business thinking. One of them is confusing correlation with causality: we tend to ascribe causality when it is only a case of correlation. To illustrate this: there was a study that said that rural women who watch Hindi serials tend to have higher aspirations and command greater respect from their husbands. The truth may be that as rural homes become more affluent, women tend to get treated better, and as a correlation, more affluent households also have televisions. A case of correlation mistaken for causation.

Another is the delusion of connecting the winning dots: academics look at a few winning companies and draw hypotheses which may not hold true outside that set of companies.

The first and what I would call the most important delusion is the 'Halo Effect Delusion'—the cognitive bias in which the perception of one quality is contaminated by a more readily available quality (for example good-looking people being rated as more intelligent). In the context of business, observers think they are making judgements about a company's customer-focus, quality of leadership or other virtues, but their judgement is contaminated by indicators of company performance such as share price or profitability. Correlations of, for example, customer-focus with business success then become meaningless, because success was the basis for the measure of customer focus.

In a literal sense clients tend to fall into the 'Halo Effect Trap', ascribing a lot of qualities to a celebrity where none may exist. They are in awe of the celebrity and often sell themselves very short. Celebrity management companies try and bridge this gap, but are often batting for the celebrity.

Celebrity mania is here to stay but if clients and agencies and talent management agencies can work together, we can organise celebrity management better.

I was not sure if I should write a chapter on celebrities, given the sensibilities of the people involved, but I realised that if they are present in 35 per cent of all the ads produced in the country, this book should at least have a few pages dedicated to lessons learnt from managing celebrities. So clearly this is a shorter chapter, but I suppose the celebrity quotient raised its relevance in your eyes as well.

Admit it, you read this chapter first. No, you didn't? Then this was, as they say in films, an 'OK Take'. Stop camera.

Doodh Si Safedi
Customer Focus

It was a typical '90s kind of busy workday at Ulka. Some people were talking on their phones, some others were peering intently at their computer screens and a couple of meetings were taking place in the meeting rooms. Suddenly, Basudev Biswas walked into my room, highly excited. I knew he had taken over the responsibility of setting up Ulka's financial advertising arm, and had been on the look-out for interesting IPOs (Initial Public Offering of shares) and financial services clients. Having worked with him for a year previously, I knew Basu's keen sense of sniffing out an opportunity.

What Basu had to tell me made me jump out of my chair in glee. The magic word he uttered was 'Nirma'. They had invited us to make a pitch!

Anyone who had anything to do with marketing in the 1980s had a healthy respect for one man and one brand. Mr Karsanbhai Patel and his creation Nirma had literally brought the multinational giant Hindustan Lever, as it was known then, to its knees.

At the Ad Asia organised in Malaysia in the year 1990 I got to listen to the legendary Marketing Director of HUL, Shunu Sen. In his presentation he singled out Karsanbhai as the person from whom he had learnt the most valuable marketing lessons, on how to tailor and market a product to the value-conscious Indian woman. Interestingly, in his presentation, he even went to the extent of saying that he considered Karsanbhai, his guru.

Karsanbhai, a chemical technologist by qualification, had formulated the innovative product himself, manufactured it in a shed and had begun by selling it from his bicycle to neighbourhood homes. But he did not stop with that. He dreamt big. He wanted to build a large company that could take on the might of the multinational consumer product giants. And what a success it was! Numerous books and case studies have been written to explain the story behind Nirma and this is a very well-known story.

Nirma was a company that evoked a great deal of respect and regard among anyone who was in marketing, more than anything else for their jingle-based, simple-format advertising, which had captured the imagination of a nation. This was the Doordarshan era and Nirma was one of the early adopters of television advertising. Their jingle was literally blasting through millions of television sets every night.

And here was Basu telling me that there was an opportunity for us to present to Karsanbhai and Nirma. We were in Ahmedabad in the next forty-eight hours to find out what the client brief was. We were told that since Nirma was getting ready to make an IPO, they wanted our skills to define a corporate mission and a corporate image campaign, as a precursor to their IPO advertising.

Our discussion with Karsanbhai and his son-in-law, Kalpeshbhai Patel was often one-sided. They spoke very little but were keen on listening to what we had to say. We told them how proud we were to have been invited to present to them and our sincere admiration for what they had achieved. We also carefully clarified that we did not work with Hindustan Lever.

As we began working on the assignment we realised that Nirma needed to define itself differently from what was seen through their simple ad. The corporation needed to be seen as having a lot more gravitas and not just as a manufacturer of economical detergent powder. When we began speaking to consumers as part of our research, we realised that most Nirma users were using a detergent powder for the first time in their lives. These were the very same consumers who had found brands like Surf unaffordable. So though advertising for the Hindustan Lever brand Wheel, a brand created to take on Nirma, spoke about 'burning hands', which was an indirect attack on Nirma, users of Nirma were quite happy with the performance of the brand. Also when we started talking to satisfied users we realised that Nirma was not just about making cheap detergents. Or cheap beauty soap (Nirma soap had been launched and was growing well at the cost of, again, Hindustan Lever brands). Nirma as visualised by Karsanbhai was clearly a great deal more than just cost economy.

We managed to create a tag line for Nirma, which we knew would be well-accepted by the investor community as well. The line, 'Better Products. Better Value. Better Living', encapsulated what Nirma stood for. It was in the business of improving the lives of Indian consumers, by offering better-value products which were of better quality. In the final analysis, Nirma users found the product of great value and thought their life had been made a little better by Nirma. They got a detergent powder that suited their purse, a detergent cake that worked better than washing soap and the beauty soap that Nirma made was also considered a great deal.

The line 'Better Products. Better Value. Better Living' was presented to Karsanbhai and we were fortunate that the planning head of the agency Ashok Aggarwal, was very fluent in Hindi and could make a one-hour presentation to Karsanbhai in Hindi, while all the slides were in English. May be it was this extra effort displayed by the agency that got Karsanbhai to talk to us about some of the new products he had in mind.

Every ad agency or anyone working in the service industry knows the best way to grow is by getting more business from a satisfied client. We now had a satisfied client as the image campaign was a success and the IPO sailed through. So when Karsanbhai started speaking about his new product ideas we were totally charged up.

Karsanbhai left us in the conference room saying that he wanted us to take a look at a new product he had in mind. We were wondering what it would be? Floor cleaner? Shampoo? Scourer? Kitchen cleaner?

But in walked Karsanbhai with tubes of Nirma Toothpaste. He asked us what we thought of the idea. Our classical brand extension do's and don'ts matrix kicked in. We started by politely saying that it was a bold move, but we were not sure. We explained how consumers are very careful about what they put in their mouth. So Nirma could go from a detergent powder to a detergent cake to a beauty soap and may be even to a shampoo, but a toothpaste was a big leap. Why would anyone buy Nirma toothpaste?

Karsanbhai had his argument ready. He explained that there was still a large segment of Indian middle and lower classes who could not afford Colgate and Nirma would fill this gap with a better product, offering better value. We requested him if we could take a few tubes of Nirma toothpaste and test them with consumers. He readily offered us a dozen tubes of his newly formulated Nirma toothpaste.

Basu, Ashok and I left the building wondering if this thing would fly with consumers. Would even a habitual Nirma washing powder user be interested in Nirma toothpaste? We knew this was a complex problem and we needed to look for answers through some innovative consumer research. Firstly, we had to use the product a few times to see how good it tasted.

The next week when we met to take stock, we all felt the product was good. Karsanbhai had made the product a little more pungent than Colgate, and it tasted a little stronger. This in our mind fitted with the overall Nirma brand promise of hard-working products. Now the question was how to take it to consumers.

Ashok suggested that we do away with the classical product test research but do some deeper immersions instead. He felt that consumers should be made to use the product in a natural setting. So a team of account planners were assigned to meet consumers as they were getting ready to brush their teeth. The target consumer was someone who was using a toothpowder and not necessarily a toothpaste. We wanted to meet and talk with at least 30 different consumers in semi-urban and rural markets and in the slums of Mumbai.

It was not too difficult to meet consumers in the morning. In many lower middle-class areas, the morning ritual of brushing one's teeth was often performed in the open. Our planners met consumers and got them to try Nirma toothpaste. Half of them were told the name before they tried it, and half were given the product in a 'masked' manner. To our surprise consumers loved the product and had no issues with the brand name 'Nirma'.

While teaching Strategic Brand Management at business schools I ask the question and invariably students opine that consumer will not accept a Nirma toothpaste and they give all the regular reasons why a brand cannot move from detergent to soap to toothpaste. But our research showed us that a brand name, for the middle and lower class consumer is nothing more than a 'stamp of quality'. To them Nirma is a good name and many consumers said, 'If it is from Nirma company it will be value for money—they will not put their name on a poor quality product.'

The research confirmed what Karsanbhai had told us. Consumers would be ready to buy a Nirma toothpaste. So off we went to Ahmedabad to meet the Nirma team and share the good news.

We were joined by Karsanbhai and we were asked to present our research findings. As we presented our findings in broken Hindi and English, we realised that Karsanbhai was not too interested in the results. As we finished we told Karsanbhai that we thought Nirma toothpaste would be a sure success.

At this stage Karsanbhai said he was dropping the toothpaste project. He then explained: 'The Nirma toothpaste as I have formulated it will be a good product and will be well-accepted by my customers. But in order to make a real impact in the market I have to price position the product in a sweet spot. If a Colgate fifty gram pack is today selling at Rs 10 to the consumer, my product cannot cost more than Rs 5 to the consumer. Since I don't have a super-efficient sales organisation, I need to give better margins to the trade, so my price to the trade cannot be more than Rs 4. That way the trade can make healthy margin even at the Rs 5 MRP. I have done my cost calculations and I cannot make the product for Rs 3. And I don't think I can sell the product for Rs 4. So the project is over.'

We realised that Karsanbhai had implemented this same strategy for all his products. He knew his consumer better than any market researcher. He knew that whatever would be the formulation, he will have to offer his product at 50 per cent of the price of the market leader. In the case of detergent powder, he had priced his Nirma washing powder at one-third the price of Surf.

Karsanbhai's razor sharp focus on his consumer made us realise that this focus was the secret of his success. As the founder and CEO of the company, he was not living in an ivory tower but was very rooted in knowing what his end consumer and the intermediaries would want. If he could not meet those expectations, he had no business to be in that business.

I was reminded of Karsanbhai's focus on understanding his consumers as I was reading the article 'Rethinking Marketing', in the *Harvard Business Review* (January-February 2010). In the article the authors speak about how companies can today interact directly with consumers and so should radically reorganise their business and put customers at the centre, instead of brands. The authors suggest that the marketing department must be reinvented as a 'customer department', the Chief Marketing Officer should be replaced by a Chief Customer Officer and product and brand managers should be made subservient to customer managers.

In his own way Karsanbhai was a Chief Customer Officer. He knew intuitively that his brand had its limitations and his customer would trust the brand only up to a point. Beyond that price limit, his customer would switch his loyalties elsewhere.

When I met Karsanbhai in early 2016 at the Nirma Management Institute, I smilingly reminding him of the Nirma Toothpaste episode. As always, Karsanbhai smiled and said, '*Success na thi*', it would not have sold.

You're Fired!

In any service industry the scariest threat you can hear is 'You're Fired!'. These words were made even more famous by Donald Trump in the television programme *Apprentice*. But what actually happens when a client says, 'I will fire your agency'? Here is an interesting long story and an even more interesting shorter one, both with a twist.

I was a young servicing executive handling this challenging client who was in a very competitive consumer product space. I was summoned by their Head of Marketing one day and when I reached the client office I was told that they had appointed a Brand Manager who would deal with the agency.

The news was a bad one on many fronts. One of the big 'highs' of working in a service industry like advertising or marketing research is that even as a low-level executive you get to meet and work with senior client professionals. This book is full of stories of how working with really smart mature thinkers makes you so much smarter. So being told that I would now have to deal with someone with my level of experience, or a little bit more, was a letdown. To add insult to injury, I learnt that the Brand Manager, who shall remain unnamed, had an advertising background. He had worked for a few years as a client service executive at a small ad agency.

In advertising it is always a challenge to have a client who has been on the other side of the business. I suppose this is the same in every service industry. It is more difficult for a bank to deal with a client who has worked in a bank. Typically, a law firm is likely have challenges dealing with a client who has worked in a law firm.

As I assimilated this piece of information, I realised that I was going to be in for a challenge. But what happened was even beyond my wildest imagination.

The Head of Marketing took me to the cubicle of the Brand Manager, made an informal introduction and left me to handle the matter at hand.

The Brand Manager made some polite noises about the campaign that had just broken, though I thought it was an outstanding campaign. Soon he started to draw some lines in the sand. He said he needed the agency to become more agile, more responsive and more proactive (words that I have heard at least a hundred times in my life in marketing/advertising). He then wanted me to create a special poster for an event being planned, date undecided. I was also told that the poster had to be presented to the Brand Manager the next day.

I tried to understand the requirement and realised that I will not be able to commit to a twenty-four hour deadline without getting the senior agency creative folks' approval. So I politely mentioned that the timeline would be a challenge and that I would get back after checking with the office (this continues to be Lesson No. 101 for young servicing executives: never commit to a deadline without checking with the powers that be).

But the Brand Manager would not accept that. He began speaking about his experience and how he, in his previous avatar, often turned around posters in a few hours for his key clients. I then had to explain that he did not work in the agency I was working in and we had strict processes and procedures, we had high quality control standards and so on. But he would not back down from his twenty-four hour demand.

Finally he used the 'F' word. No, not the one you are thinking about. He said, 'I will fire you, if you don't agree to this!'

Then, I don't know what happened to me. Something snapped inside. I was too young, too naïve, may be too idealistic. Maybe I was too arrogant.

I decided to go on the offensive. I retorted heatedly, 'You cannot fire me, even if you want to. Just as I cannot fire you even if I wanted to. In fact your father can't fire me. Only your grandfather can fire me. So don't make empty threats. I am leaving your office. See what you can do.'

I realise now while writing this that I had overstepped my limits. I had no business lashing out at a valuable client. But for some strange reason the reverse threat worked like a charm. The Brand Manager suddenly realised that he had no business threatening the agency which had been hired a year earlier and had done great work. In fact, the agency's track record was known to all his superiors. Even if he had wanted he may not have been able to 'fire' us.

The Brand Manager got up from his chair and stopped me from leaving. His tone changed and he asked me to sit down and have a cup of tea. We realised that both of us had said things that we had no business saying. Finally we agreed to me 'trying my best to meet the deadline'. As it turned out I delivered a great poster in forty-eight hours.

I use this story in all the client servicing training sessions I handle to explain how in this instance both the client and the servicing executives went beyond what they were permitted to say. One should not threaten to fire someone and if one gets threatened, lashing out is a bad idea.

The lesson on how to handle a 'fired' threat came back to me from a story I heard about an office attendant in the Bangalore office of the agency.

This office attendant was not the most efficient nor the most hard-working. But he was loyal to the agency. He knew everyone well and always had a smile on his lips. The story goes that one afternoon, around 4 p.m., a young client servicing executive wanted the office attendant to rush to a client office and deliver a parcel before the client office closed. The office attendant told the young executive that he would not be able to do it because there was not enough time and he had something personal to do at 5.30 p.m. On hearing this answer the young hot-tempered executive told the attendant, 'You are fired!' When the office attendant heard the word, he did not lash out at the young executive. It seems he told the executive that he should wait a bit in his seat and that he would get a call. He should implement his action after taking the call.

The office attendant, I am told, rushed to the next office and spoke with the owner of that office (this incident predates mobile phones, emails and social media). A call was made. And within an hour the young executive got a call from Mumbai, from the Chairman's office. The Chairman told the young executive, 'Young man, you cannot fire a peon on a whim. Please don't threaten a person who has no other means of livelihood. Call him and speak with him. He will take care of your request.'

I don't have to tell you what happened. The young executive did not realise that the office attendant had spent a decade in the company. He did not know that the neighbour was a dear friend of the Chairman of the agency. And the neighbour had stepped in to speak with the Chariman about the 'firing' and got the Chairman to make an urgent call to the servicing executive.

These two stories present interesting questions about where to draw the line and how to react to a threat. As a frontline sales person we face these questions all the time. It was possible for me to accept the twenty-four hour deadline and leave the client office. I could have got back to him the next day saying that I would need another day. But that would have created a new set of problems. The office attendant could have broken down and cried; or could have taken the package and left the office for home.

The two situations presented were relatively harmless. I have heard of more horrifying stories of client demands, some rude and some impolite. Sometimes, it may even include demands for bribes in cash or kind. Once you accede to such a demand, you have drawn a new line in the sand.

I have experienced clients asking for refunds and rebates in cash by dangling the carrot of 'more business'. Where do you draw the line and how do you say no. Thanks to well-laid down practices and processes, we always said, 'No, thank you. We will settle for the small carrot.'

In his book *How Will You Measure Your Life*, Prof. Clayton Christensen addresses personal issues we face all the time in our professional and personal lives. He believes that each of us should have a personal moral line and if we believe that moral line is important, we should stick to that line 100 per cent of the time. He explains that it is easier to stick to it 100 per cent of the time than to adhere to it 98 per cent of the time. I think the bigger point made was that once you let go and say that 2 per cent of the time you will accede to unreasonable demands, it will eventually creep up to 5 per cent and soon 25 per cent of the time.

Prof. Christensen offers a few more useful tips in his highly readable little book. He feels it starts with a family culture, and I think in the work environment, it depends on the culture of the organisation, as set by the senior leadership team. In fact, Prof. Christensen says what parents 'don't do for you' matter as much as what they 'do for you'. The time to build a strong relationship is when it seems least important (if someone you know is in a tough spot, that is the time to reach out to him; he may not call you out of fear of being rebuked, but you can call him).

Getting fired is a rather scary thought, both for you as a professional and for the firm you represent. But if you approach the F word with a lot of fear you will lose the battle before it has even begun. What you believe as the grand strategy or the big vision for the firm is actually made up of many small every day decisions. If you don't live up to the vision every day, you will end up slipping down the slope, rather speedily.

Don't get overly psyched by the F-word. If you have the self-confidence, you can convert the negative 'F word' into a positive 'F word' like Fantastic, Fun or Future.

Decisions Made Rapidly

How long does it take to have a new campaign on air after you win an account? If you are in financial services, how long will it take to finish the deal and disburse a multi-million dollar loan? And if you are in IT services, how long will it take for you to finalise the details of your assignment, before your team can start working on the information architecture?

The answers will vary, I am sure. But in advertising it is very rare that an agency wins a new account and manages to get a spanking new television commercial out on air in just three weeks. Or was it two weeks, I forget. But in my long career in advertising and marketing, I have never had the occasion of creating an ad and having it on air in three weeks, except once. And that is an interesting story.

It was a big global win. The FCB team had managed to pitch and win the Compaq account (before it was bought by Hewlett Packard, but more about that later) and the agency had told the client that their Indian arm, FCB Ulka would be able to take on the assignment with immediate effect.

I was soon off to Bangalore to meet the client. The Marketing

Communication Chief turned out to be an old IIT friend, Bringi Dev, who got us to meet with the head of the PC business, Ravi Swaminathan.

Ravi was clear about his requirements. He told us that he had a new range of Compaq Pressario computers ready to be launched. The feature he wanted us to highlight were the changeable 'bezels'. The computer was sold with three coloured bezels, so you could make the computer look blue, green or red. This was in a sense Compaq's answer to the tantalisingly coloured iMac computers that had been rolled out by Apple. We were shocked to hear that Ravi wanted to get the television ads out on air as fast as possible, maybe in a couple of weeks. We said we would try, but were not sure we would be able to do anything that fast.

To appreciate the complexities of the advertising film production business, you need to understand how the whole process works. First the client briefs the agency. Often the brief is very sketchy. The agency planning team gets to work on the brand, does its own research to help discover consumer insights into what would appeal to the buying public. The client is then met again so that the agency and the client reach an agreement on what should be the 'Single Minded Propositon' or SMP and what would be the 'Reason to Believe' or RTB. In the case of Compaq we decided that we would not question the brief given by the client, a rarity for the agency those days, but would stick to what was given as the brief by the client: changeable colourful bezels to make the using of a PC more fun.

Once the brief is agreed upon, the creative team gets to work on the brief to develop ideas that can make the boring SMP/RTB come alive in front of the consumer. The process of getting from a brief to a good script could take a few days to a few weeks depending on how excited the creative team gets after the briefing meeting.

Then the script is presented to the client who may want changes. Or may outright reject the ad, often changing the brief, SMP and RTB.

Once the script crosses the client hurdle, it finds its way into the film department of the agency. The Films Manager, normally a diva of sorts, reads the script and decides which film director will do justice to the script (the Creative Director on the brand may have his favourite director and that adds another dimension to this story). The director is often emailed the script. He or she may be out at a shoot or holidaying in the Bahamas, but this cat-and-mouse game goes on till the director says he is interested. Often, it is not just one director. So the same process is repeated. The film department then tries to obtain a quotation from the film company that is producing the film, often run by said director's wife or brother. Haggling begins, which sometimes reaches absurd proportions. In the interim, the selected director's work (show reel) is shared with the client. Clients are also sometimes known to suggest new names, based on who had done their previous ad films or what they saw on television the previous night.

Finally, the director is frozen. The budget is approved. The big day then arrives. No not to show the film but for the 'Pre Production Meeting' (PPM for short). These PPMs can themselves last a day. Some clients insist on the director sharing a very, very detailed description of the film, including details like the pen stand on the table on which the computer would be placed, the watch the model in the film would be wearing, etc. One big hurdle is the finalisation of the models to be used in the film. This can throw everything into a tailspin.

If the PPM goes well, the director is now cleared for take off. Literally. An exotic location is chosen for the shoot and a whole troop of people from the agency and even the client organisation fly off to Thailand, or Malaysia or South Africa for the shoot.

After the shoot is over, the editing, music recording and remixing could take a few days to a few weeks. Sometimes, the music director we want is not available for two weeks, sometimes it could be something else.

Then the film is presented to the client who may want changes and we go through the loop all over again.

You may wonder why I took you on a rather long course on the madness we call TV ad production. It was with a purpose. You will soon realise.

Coming back to the Compaq story, we heard that Ravi was going to be in Mumbai four days after our first briefing meeting and wanted to know if we could present our preliminary ideas. The team assigned to work on the brand, Ramesh Ravindernath and Mahender Bheda were highly charged up and agreed immediately.

The script presented to Ravi went something as follows. The film opens in a large office. Our young man is working on his computer when he spots a lovely-looking girl walking towards him. She is dressed in a blue jacket. He wants to impress her and so he changes the bezel of his Compaq Pressario to blue, muttering to himself, 'What a co-incidence you are wearing blue.' Just as he completes the makeover of his computer, he realises that the girl has taken off her blue jacket and she is now dressed in a red shirt. So he quickly removes the blue bezels and switches them to red, but when she finally reached his desk, she is dressed in a green t-shirt. And he goes, 'What a co-incidence ... oohhh.' The product story kicks in.

Ravi loved the film, but had a big problem with the situation. He wanted to position the brand for home use and not office use. And he wanted Preity Zinta as the attractive girl in the ad. When can you come back, was the final question asked of the agency.

The team came back to office thinking they had to rework the film and did not know how to crunch the time. As we discussed the script in detail, we realised that the same story could be told even from a home setting. The boy could be working in the veranda of a bungalow, the girl could be parking her cycle and walking up the driveway and the drama could unfold in the veranda. The creative team working on the film had to be shown a house (in a photograph) where such a thing could happen.

Much to Ravi's surprise the team was back at his office in less than twenty-four hours with the newly polished script. Being a Delhi native, Ravi could instantly visualise the sequence of events. He was, however, a little disappointed that his budget could not get him Preity Zinta or any other film star.

In the next twenty-four hours the film manager had located a film maker who was free and keen on doing the film. The PPM was held forty-eight hours after the script was approved by the client.

Ravi cleared the treatment of the film and the budget.

In four days the film was ready for presentation to the client. And it went on air just two days later.

If you do the math you will realise that the whole process was completed in less than three weeks, in fact in less than two weeks.

This miracle was partly due to serendipity. The film director who could do justice was available at short notice (Sabal Shekhawat). The models or talent the film director wanted were also available. The location was available. The cinematographer was available. And there were no rains, strikes, floods, etc. But there was yet another big factor that enabled this miracle to happen.

Ravi Swaminathan approached the agency with a lot of trust. It helped that one of his closest friends happened to be a director of the agency. He gave a clear brief and was forthright in giving feedback when he saw the first script. He did not want the agency to show him multiple options. He was happy with a script that the agency recommended.

Once the script met his requirement, except for the Priety Zinta request which I think was in jest, he left the agency alone to do its job. The process of approving the models, the location, even the budget was smooth. There was no army of brand managers getting into every line of the script and quotation.

We at the agency were not really sure Ravi wanted the film in a hurry (by the way, every client who hires a new agency says, 'I want the new campaign like yesterday!'). So when we breezed through all the hurdles, we did not know if we were awake or dreaming.

When the film was finally presented to Ravi, he approved it without a single change. Again a rarity. The ad went on air and gave a big boost to Compaq's Diwali sales. The film was so well-liked by the Asia Pacific team of Compaq that they took it to other Asian counties.

An ad that was created from scratch in just two weeks.

I should admit there have been a few other examples where clients gave rapid approvals and campaigns rolled out in a few weeks. But most campaigns take a few months to see the light of day. The Compaq tale demonstrates that when you have a client who knows his mind, is very clear on what he is looking for, even a big budget ad film can be delivered in two weeks.

In the article 'What Sets Successful CEOs Apart', in the *Harvard Business Review* (May–June 2017) researchers Elena Lytkina Botelho, Kim Rosenkoetter Powell, Stephen Kincaid and Dina Wang point out that too many CEOs fail in their jobs because there is a fundamental disconnect between what the board of directors think makes for an ideal CEO and what actually leads to high performance. They have identified four specific behaviours that prove critical to their performance: decisiveness, engagement for impact, adapting proactively, and delivering reliably. The first and possibly most critical skill is the ability to decide with speed and conviction. High performance

CEOs also know that wrong decisions are often better than no decision at all.

The Compaq Pressario story taught me that when you have a client who is clear about what he wants, a miracle is within reach and can happen. Like a fully finished TV ad in just two weeks.

Value Quality
Over Cost

What happens to the costs that your vendor partner incurs? Where does it get added to your bills? Have you ever wondered about the implications of these hidden costs?

We got a lesson on cost management some years ago from someone who knows more about this than any of us—Mr Azim Premji.

Our agency had been working on the Wipro Consumer Care division from the late '80s and there was a great deal of mutual respect and regard between the agency and the client. This led us to being called to work on the corporate advertising account of Wipro in 1998.

As Wipro's business had started to change dramatically in the late '90s, the company had engaged a famous designer, Shombit Sengupta to revisualise what the company should stand for. After much consumer and customer research done across the country, the company decided to go with the 'Rainbow Flower' logo created by Shombit with the tag line 'Applying Thought' (the company has gone in for a new identity since, in 2017).

We were tasked with creating an advertising campaign to promote the new logo and to link it to the various aspects of the businesses of Wipro. The first campaign the agency team created was presented to Mr Premji and the consumer products marketing team. While the response from Mr Premji was positive, it was dismissed by some of the other key members of the Wipro IT leadership team.

To be fair, some of the most difficult ad campaigns to sell to a client are corporate campaigns. For one, there is no real metric to measure if it works or fails. Secondly, there is no single divisional head or divisional marketing head who owns such campaigns and therefore wants to see it out so that he can get an uptick on his sales numbers. Finally, the CEO often seeks the opinion of so many team members that it is a miracle if a campaign can get past the gate in a year. Jokes aside, I know for a fact that agencies have worked on corporate campaigns for months without them leaving the agency studios.

This case, though, was a little different. Since there was a new logo being unveiled, there was some urgency around the campaign and there was a need felt to communicate with a larger audience about the new Wipro.

After two attempts we managed to create a campaign that was liked by almost everyone. Mr Premji wanted some small changes to be made and the campaign was re-presented to him in Bangalore. For some strange reason I could not make the trip to Bangalore and Mr Premji was kind enough to allow one of my senior colleagues, Santosh Menon, to travel to Bangalore and present the final versions of the campaign.

Remember, the campaigns could have been sent by courier or email (which had just about started making its presence felt), but good clients and good agencies prefer a face-to-face meeting, especially when the matter under discussion is creative.

Mr Premji's office had confirmed a 5 p.m. meeting on a Friday and Santosh had planned his Bangalore trip accordingly.

The meeting went exactly as planned. The six ads were discussed threadbare and the body copy was also agreed upon. When the meeting ended it was 8 p.m.

It was then that Mr Premji politely asked Santosh, 'You are from the Mumbai office of the agency, aren't you? When are you heading back?'

Santosh replied that he was planning to take a morning flight back to Mumbai the next day (Saturday).

Mr Premji interjected, 'Why are you spending the night in Bangalore? I know there is a 10.30 p.m. flight to Mumbai. My office can book you a seat right now!'

Santosh, smiled and thanked Mr Premji and said that he would figure out a way back to Mumbai quickly.

As Santosh narrated the incident to me the following Monday, he even mentioned that Mr Premji had even dialled the airport booking office of the airline (secretly, I think that was Santosh's imagination getting the better of him, but that's another story). What he told me and he did not tell Mr Premji was this. He had been planning on meeting up with some of his old Mumbai friends, now in Bangalore, and go on a late-night pub crawl.

The incident stuck in my head. Not the pub crawl but the fact that Mr Premji suggested that Santosh head back the same night. Why did Mr Premji ask Santosh about his return trip? How is that he was aware of the late night flight? And what lessons can that teach us?

A decade later at a Board lunch meeting in Navi Mumbai, the topic of the cost consciousness of WalMart came up. 'Kas' Kasturirangan who is one of the most revered marketing leaders this country has produced, narrated an interesting insight into how WalMart managed its vendor relationships. They were focused on helping their vendors manage their costs better and were open to helping their vendors, if they were willing to share their costs.

One other cardinal rule that WalMart followed was that all the vendors, or should we say Principals, who fly down to the WalMart head office at Bentonville Arizona, are politely pushed to fly out the same night and not stay the night at Bentonville. They are expected to fly into Bentonville in the morning and fly out the same evening. Meetings are all scheduled to end in such a way that visiting executives can fly out the same evening.

We got talking about this and realised that WalMart did not want its suppliers to spend money on hotel and overnight stay because they realised that all these extra costs incurred would finally be loaded on to the cost of the material and get billed to WalMart and to its end customer. So not only was WalMart careful about looking at stuff like raw material costs, they were also acutely conscious about the overhead costs of even their vendors.

Thanks to these lessons, I have maintained a habit of minimising overnight stay at hotels and prefer a morning-evening trip if that can be managed. I should admit that with airports now located far from the heart of cities like Bangalore and Delhi Gurugram, this is becoming a challenge. I also realise that an overnight stay adds other costs to the trip in addition to the hotel cost; the cost of the taxi for the next day, meals, etc.

Business Class travel is yet another habit one did not get into, thanks to the lessons learnt from clients like Wipro. And this habit was percolated right through the organisation and it was embraced with a lot of conviction, not just as a diktat from the CEO.

The Economic Times once had an interesting article entitled '7 Lessons from Frugal Habits of the Rich'. Six of those lessons were:

1. They live below their means.
2. They spend less on clothes, shoes and food.
3. They save and invest first and spend later.
4. They don't carry much cash and use credit cards wisely.

5. They look for discounts, coupons, and other ways to cut costs.
6. They value quality over cost.

A seventh lesson that I found surprising was that they also give lesser percentage of their income to charity. I am not sure if that is a 'lesson' in the true sense of the term, but that was what was mentioned in the article.

The article also profiled what they call the 'Thrifty Rich Club'. Quite naturally, Mr Premji featured prominently in the list, as did Warren Buffett, N. R. Narayana Murthy, Mark Zuckerberg and even Rajnikant, the Tamil superstar.

While outlining Mr Premji's habits, they mentioned that he flew economy class and didn't stay in flashy hotels and drove modest cars like the Ford Escort. Unlike the seventh 'lesson' though, he has earmarked 39 per cent of his stake in Wipro (worth about Rs 50,000 crores) to a charitable trust.

I sometimes wonder if such strong focus on cost control can be counter-productive to an organisational culture. For example, a company cannot allow cost to dictate its safety or health standards. Better-run companies ensure that all women employees get company-arranged taxi cab service when they travel. Some companies insist that executives should travel business class if the length of travel is over four hours.

Obviously, there are many factors that need to be considered as one lays down policies and those may not all point in the direction of 'low costs'. But nevertheless, a focus on costs is important. What one needs to remember is that what can be dismissed as a small cost item, can in fact balloon into a significant cost, in the bigger scheme of things.

So if you can fly back the same night, please do. It is also likely that you will be able to sleep better on your own soft bed.

The Self-Driven Driver

It was my first trip to the Hyderabad branch of the agency. I was met at the airport by Ram Seshu, the branch manager. In his own style, Ram introduced me to the car driver, 'Ambi, this is Ghousebhai, the company driver. He is much more than a driver, as you will soon discover.' I politely smiled at Ghousebhai and got into the car.

In the office we got down to reviewing the business and soon Ghousebhai walked in with a tray, carrying our tea. While I was a little surprised, I hid it well and thanked him. And as soon as he left the room I asked Ram, 'Wasn't that your driver, Ram?' to which Ram smiled and replied, 'I told you.'

We left it at that and continued with the meeting. I assumed that Ghousebhai was trying to impress the new boss and so was going beyond the call of duty to score a few extra brownie points.

My trips to Hyderabad continued and during each trip I was met by Ghousebhai (the courtesy of being met by the Branch Manager at the airport was an overkill that the agency strongly discouraged; rightly so, I should add).

A year or so later, when Vijay Kumar took over as Branch Director, I noticed Ghousebhai helping out in the studio. As some older readers acquainted with the ad industry and its workings may know and recall, during the '90s an agency was defined by its studio. It consisted of artists who did line and half-tone illustrations, made layouts, ordered typesetting, did a cut-paste of those typesets into layouts, etc. I spotted Ghousebhai doing a cut-paste job in the studio. Clearly, Ghousebhai was multi-faceted. In fact, Vijay jokingly said that he sometimes wondered when Ghousebhai would take over the branch manager's cabin.

It is difficult to manage an agency in Hyderabad if you don't have a couple of large, what you may call 'anchor clients'. After running a loss-making branch for almost a decade, the agency decided to shut the Hyderabad office in the 2000s. The staff strength had come down to less than ten and I had the painful task of speaking with each of the team members. Remember, I must have been to the office more than a hundred times in the previous fifteen years. While some of the staff were new, some like Ghousebhai, had been a constant feature. As an organisation we did realise that the staff whom we were letting go had nothing to do with the success or otherwise of the branch. So the company decided to offer all of them alternative employment in any of the other offices of the agency. None of them wanted the transfer though, and were quite happy to accept the one-time severance package that had been put together by the agency.

The last conversation I had was with Ghousebhai. I was worried that it would be a tough conversation. Ghousebhai was on the company rolls and therefore enjoyed privileges that were not easy to come by. Most companies had stopped employing drivers on their payroll and so a 'company driver' was a true mark of honour.

My conversation with Ghousebhai was probably the easiest that I had that day. He said he understood the situation the company faced. He had known about the performance of the branch and realised that it had been a loss-making office for many years. This event, in his mind, was overdue. I asked him what he planned to do and he said he had a few options and would figure out something. I told him that I had friends in town who may want to use his services, but he smiled and declined the offer.

Later I heard that he decided to buy an auto-rickshaw and drive it himself.

When I was in Hyderabad in early 2017 to deliver a book talk at the Advertising Club, I was delighted to see Ghousebhai. He had dropped by (with his old colleague Rajkumar) to say hello to me. I asked him how he was, how his family was doing and whether he was still driving an auto. He smiled and said that he had saved well and owned a few properties that yielded good rental income. His driving days were behind him. I thanked him for coming to see me and invited him to join us for dinner. He mentioned that it was the Ramzan month and he had broken his fast and had already had his 'Iftar' meal. But he was happy to have seen me after a gap of over fifteen years!

Ghosebhai was a driver, but he was also a lot more. Instead of sitting in the car and gossiping with other drivers (or watching inane movies on mobile phones, the latest affliction of unemployed or underemployed India), he made himself useful in many ways. Nobody asked him to double up as the office peon or the studio assistant. But he made sure he productively used every minute of his time at work. Needless to add, he was the most popular person in the office. Always smiling and ready to do your bidding. I suspect if he had been given the opportunity to study he would have made a terrific branch manager.

My good friend Madhya Sadanand Shetty started life as a dispatch clerk at Boots Company at the age of eighteen. He completed his graduation and MBA as he continued to work at Boots. He was accommodated in the Marketing department as a clerical assistant, where he proved to be better than all the others, moved to brand management, then to sales management and finally retired as General Manager-Sales. I am proud to claim that we were colleagues for six years in the '80s.

What makes some of your team members reach for the stars and perform way beyond their role? What makes most others stay within the narrow job description?

I remember a client, let us call him Ramu, at a large company who had been in his marketing position for over a month. I saw that his table was empty. Not a bit of paper or notebook or even a pen (before you get to the wrong conclusion, this was before the age of the internet and laptop). I asked him how come he had such a clean table. He replied that he had 'requisitioned' for stationery and the admin department was yet to give him what he needed. So he had a clean table and had not written a word for the past one month. That company did not go far, neither did this person.

What makes one employee become a Ghousebhai or a Shetty, while many stay at the same level as Ravi? What should an organisation do to encourage the Ghousebhais?

Stephen Covey's book *7 Habits of Highly Effective People* is probably the most widely read and quoted management book of the last decade. I was happy to note that Ghousebhai, who probably has not read a single management book in his life, embodied some of the principles enunciated in the 7 Habits Book.

Start with the first one: Be Proactive. Ghousebhai did not wait for someone to tell him to help around the office. He made himself more useful, by being proactive. Interestingly, he managed to do this without ruffling the feathers of his fellow employees.

The second habit: Begin with the end in mind. Ghousebha's end was to help the organisation. Unlike Ramu, he was not one to wait for the organisation to supply the pen and paper. Ghousebhai wanted the company to succeed and was willing to do whatever was in his capacity to help.

The other habits Stephen Covey puts down are: Put First Things First; Think Win-Win; Seek First to Understand, then be Understood; Synergise; and Sharpen the Saw.

There are many Ghousebhais around us. Do we know them? What can we do to recognise them—give them a little pat, a smile, a wave? How can we create more Ghousbhais? And what will happen if an organisation is full of Ghousebhais? What will happen to this country if all drivers instead of watching inane videos all day, become proactively useful?

Self-driven cars can wait. What we perhaps need are more self-driven drivers.

One Final Squeeze!

Dr B. J. Prashantam heads the Institute for Human Relations, Counselling and Psychotherapy at Christian Medical College (CMC), Vellore. His sessions at the Coaching Federation of India's CEO Certification programme were some of the most enjoyable times I have had in a seminar/workshop in a very long while. In his own modest, almost self-effacing style, Dr Prashantam narrates stories that embed in them valuable lessons. He narrated the following story to us, on how our lives could be so much more enjoyable if only we 're-frame' what is happening around us.

Apparently, this middle-aged man had approached Dr Prashantam with a complaint that he was being verbally abused by his wife, almost every day. As soon as he got home, his wife would start with her tirade about how miserable her life was, how she had to listen to her mother-in-law's multifarious demands, how the children were intolerable, how he was not helping her in any way and so on. This often got the man into a nasty mood, provoking an angry reaction, leading to an escalation of the war of words.

Dr Prashantam's suggestion to this patient was to listen to whatever his wife said, without reacting. The technique, Dr Prashantam explained, was not to listen to the words but to the tone, the inflection, the flow, the voice timbre, the intonation, the pauses, the dramatic changes in voice quality, facial expressions, movement of eyes, eyebrows and more. The patient was not sure what Dr Prashantam meant, but said he would try.

At the next counselling session, held a month later, the patient arrived a changed man. He explained how he was now focusing on the flow of the tirade and not on the words and discovered that his wife had a great voice. Her diction was fantastic. Her voice quality was melodious and her dramatic delivery was also something he had started to admire. As he focused on the voice and not the words, he too was not reacting to her, the way he used to. The tirade therefore did not last the usual one hour but ended in thirty minutes (just as he was getting used to enjoying it). He reported a dramatic improvement in his marital relations. Even his mother had become less demanding in the aftermath.

Dr Prashantam explained how we could change the context by creating a new frame of reference. In negotiations this is called 'Re-Framing'. The situation you are in, when it is re-framed, starts looking very different. What seemed like a lost cause suddenly starts looking salvageable. Just as the man's daily verbal battle with his wife.

In a very similar way, we can all re-frame our own reactions to what our client says. Irrespective of the industry we operate in, whether it is the service industry or manufacturing, B2B or B2C, we face clients every day, sometimes more than once a day. How can we re-frame these interactions, to make them more enjoyable and may be even more informative and educational?

In this book I have presented around twenty-five odd stories of client interactions. The common thread to these interactions was that in each of these instances I ended up learning something new. It was not as if my clients were trying to teach me new things. But by observing what they did, what they said and how they behaved in the situation at hand, I ended up learning a lot. By applying the S.P.O.N.G.E. framework.

So whichever industry you are in, be it financial services, hospitality, advertising, information technology, engineering services, chemicals, entertainment, etc., you are bound to get an opportunity to meet interesting people. Some who are a lot more educated and a lot wiser than you. Some who may be younger than you and a lot more dynamic. Some who are very good at what they do and are at the peak of their professions. Some who are ordinary, everyday people, but with some extraordinary qualities. Each one of them can help you in some way or the other.

A tip about a new book to read. A new place to visit. A new way to approach a situation. A new way to address a problem. The lessons could be endless.

I hope the book has opened your eyes to the joys of being a 'Sponge' and soaking it all up. As you navigate your own career in sales, marketing or client servicing, you too can become more effective in your job, if you can imbibe some 'sponge-like' qualities.

Instead of approaching each client as a necessary evil to be dealt with, imagine the possibilities if you see each interaction as an opportunity to learn. As you enjoy the customer interactions, you too will figure out how you can become better and better every day, absorbing all the life-giving nutrients, like a sponge deep on the ocean floor.

I was able to literally 're-frame' my interactions with clients, some tough, some nice, some surprising, into mini coaching and mentoring sessions.

Let me remind you once again about the S.P.O.N.G.E. Learning Framework before I leave you to your spongy devices: S – Super Active listening; P – Probe and Question; O – Observe and Note; N – New Behaviour to Emulate; G – Get to a Goal; E – Expand, Enlarge, Share.

Sponge it up, I say ... with a smile!

Suggested Reading

1. *Practice of Management*, Peter Drucker
2. *Fifth Discipline*, Peter Senge
3. *Moment of Truth*, Jan Carlzon
4. *The Hero & The Outlaw*, Margaret Mark and Carol Pearsons
5. *Mavericks at Work*, William C. Taylor and Polly Labarre
6. *Start-Up Nation: The Story of Israel's Economic Miracle*, Dan Senor and Saul Singer
7. *Flying Without a Net*, Thomas J. Delong
8. *Learning in Action*, David A. Garwin
9. *Man's Search for Meaning*, Viktor E. Frankl
10. *Flow*, Mihaly Csikszentemihalyi
11. *The Tao of Coaching*, Max Landsberg
12. *Blue Ocean Strategy*, W. Chan Kim and Renée Mauborgne
13. *50 Rules to Keep a Client Happy*, Fred Poppe
14. *Discover Your True North*, Bill George
15. *Authentic Happiness*, Martin Seligman
16. *The Power of Story*, Jim Loehr
17. *Leading Change*, John Kotter
18. *Originals*, Adam Grant
19. *The Halo Effect*, Phil Rosensweig
20. *How Will You Measure Your Life*, Clayton Christensen
21. *The 7 Habits of Highly Effective People*, Stephen Covey

Acknowledgements

This book is a result of a discussion that I started with my friend and literary agent Anish Chandy two years ago, soon after the publication of my last book (*Nawabs Nudes Noodles: India Through 50 Years of Advertising*). As we got talking I mentioned how I was lucky to have worked with so many wonderful clients who had taught me so much. The agencies I worked in, first the short stint at Rediffusion Advertising and later a twenty-five year plus innings at FCB Ulka, were both agencies blessed with a great roster of clients.

Folklore has it that in ad agencies clients are both revered and cursed. Revered because they pay the bill. Cursed because they are often stumbling blocks for good ideas. I am sure the same sentiment is shared in most service oriented industries.

Fortunately for me, the agencies and the long-term clients I worked with believed in a 'agency-client partnership', where opinions are shared freely without fear.

The stories in the book are not all from my own personal experience, they also include what I heard from my colleagues at FCB Ulka including Anil Kapoor, Arvind Wable, Shashi Sinha, Niteen Bhagwat, Nagesh Alai and others. You will meet many of them in the book. So my first thanks goes to all these wonderful people who shared their 'Sponge' stories with me.

I would like to thank my literary agent, Anish Chandy and my editor Karthik Venkatesh who did a great job in managing my various demands, editing the contents and crafting the project. Gautam Padmanabhan and Krishnakumar Nair of Westland have been big pillars of support. Special thanks to Saurav Das for a stunning cover design. The Westland team's inputs right through the project has been truly very helpful.

All my books start off with my wife Nithya critically going through the first draft to point out errors. So thanks to her for her patience and perseverance.

This book is a result of what I have managed to learn or should I say 'Sponge' from all my clients and the stories I heard from my colleagues. Every Sponge story is a close-to-true narration of what happened. If you find the stories of value, the credit should go to the clients mentioned in the book. The faults are entirely my own.